Thomas Merton and the Individual Witness

Thomas Merton and the Individual Witness

Kingdom Making in a Post-Christian, Post-Truth World

David E. Oberson

The Lutterworth Press

The Lutterworth Press
P.O. Box 60
Cambridge
CB1 2NT
United Kingdom

www.lutterworth.co
publishing@lutterworth.co

Paperback ISBN: 978 0 7188 9770 3
PDF ISBN: 978 0 7188 9769 7

British Library Cataloguing in Publication Data
A record is available from the British Library

First published by Cascade Books, 2022

This edition published by The Lutterworth Press, 2024,
by arrangement with Wipf and Stock Publishers

Copyright © David E. Oberson, 2022

All rights reserved. No part of this edition may be reproduced, stored electronically or in any retrieval system, or transmitted in any form or by any means, electronic, mechanical, photocopying, recording, or otherwise, without prior written permission from the Publisher (permissions@lutterworth.co).

To Olivia and Beth

Contents

Acknowledgments | ix

Introduction | 1

1. Where Are We and How Did We Get Here? | 5
2. Post-Truth | 30
3. Why Merton? | 41
4. Merton and the Individual Witness, Part I | 74
5. Merton and the Individual Witness, Part II | 95

Conclusion | 118

Bibliography | 121

Index | 127

Acknowledgments

I AM BLESSED TO have such a great family and friends. My parents Bill and Nancy, gave me a lifetime of unconditional love and support. My brother Will has always been my hero, and I am grateful for his love and friendship. He and his wife Lea Lynn created a wonderful family, and I am so proud of Katie and Scott, Maddie and Chris, and Allie and Jeff.

Thanks to all of the Milfords: Rob, Judy, Chris, Krissy, McCall, Phil, Forrest, Atherton, Robby, Edyee, Addison, Maddie, Skye, Will, Adrian, Jack, Owen, Sadie, and Maggie for welcoming me into their family.

David and Jill Meckle, David and Ann Barnett, and Doug and Lee Ann Galligan have been friends for decades, and my life is better because of it.

I am grateful to Shawn Proctor and Tom Malewitz for their friendship and encouragement during the long process of writing this short book.

My daughter Olivia has been my *raison d'etre* since the day she was born. It has been such a pleasure watching her grow into being a strong, brilliant, and compassionate educator. She and her wonderful husband Nick exemplify all that is good in their generation.

And finally, thanks to my dear wife Beth. She is the love of my life, my best friend, and she makes me a better person.

Introduction

OVER SIXTY YEARS AGO, Thomas Merton—monk, mystic, and writer—proclaimed that we are living in a post-Christian world. That is, the influence of the institutional church is in decline and the popular version of Christianity presented to society has in many ways become a caricature of itself. Merton did not have a defeatist attitude about this trend. Instead, he saw it as an opportunity for Christians to engage with the world in a new way; one that was not reliant on the historic size and stature of the church. More importantly, Merton believed that in the coming years the individual Christian would play a vital role, presenting the reality and message of Christ to a world that was increasingly indifferent to it.

Since that time, the religious landscape has continued to change, with the number of Christians steadily shrinking. While that trend is not new, we have reached a tipping point. In recent surveys, the number of people who identify as "None," someone with no particular religious affiliation, outnumbers the combined total of all Mainline Protestants. In addition, research into the beliefs of religious teens shows that most of these young people either don't know or care what their faiths teach. Instead, they profess a belief in a God that is "on call," ready to aid us in a time of crisis, but who otherwise leaves us alone to live our lives. This is a God that prioritizes our subjective well-being without any calls to sacrifice in order to serve others.

All of these religious changes are occurring in a broader post-truth culture in which facts matter less and less, and our society is increasingly divided. This is easily seen in the devolution of our political system into bitter tribalism. While our nation has always been factional, we have entered a new era where beating the other side is more important than advocating for a particular issue, candidate, or course of action. We live in a time when it is difficult for people to even agree on the basic facts to be interpreted and debated.

Technology has taken the inherent tendency towards sectarianism and propelled it to a whole new level. The internet, social media, talk radio, and cable news now make it possible to burrow further into our own point of view, surrounding ourselves with "news" that reinforces our own position. There is no longer a need to enter the marketplace of ideas. Instead, we can stay within the calcified walls of our own opinions, fortifying them with like-minded ones.

Percolating beneath it all is a pervasive kind of anti-intellectualism that in many ways contributes to and propels these forces. The masses are implored not to "be sheep"—we should not listen to expert advice but instead should follow our heart and do our own internet "research." This is more than just healthy skepticism; it is an assault on the very concept of expertise itself. As a result, alternative facts and even alternative science now proliferate online. Facebook and YouTube contain thousands of pages and videos that promote these points of view, with many clips receiving millions of views. In them, creationism is elevated to Creation Science, pre-COVID anti-vaxers point to their own "facts" to argue against children being vaccinated against life-threatening illnesses, and conspiracy theories from the Flat Earth to QAnon prosper.

A number of prominent Christians have written popular books addressing how the faithful should respond to our post-Christian and post-truth world. However, most dwell on various elements of the culture war with much hand wringing about the fraying of our country's moral fabric, and present a dystopian vision of the future of Christianity. Some declare that Christians are under attack from secular society, writing that "today Christians are the most persecuted and harassed religious community in the world"[1] and that things are so dire "the light of Christianity is flickering out all over the West. There are people alive today who may live to see the effective death of Christianity within our civilization."[2] Many are fixated on sexuality, and homosexuality in particular. The rights of Christians, it is argued, have been subordinated to those of the gay community, with the Supreme Court's ruling on same-sex marriage being the "Waterloo" of the culture war.[3] One prominent Christian writer is concerned that today gay

---

1. Chaput, *Strangers in a Strange Land*, 214.
2. Dreher, *Benedict Option*, 8.
3. Dreher, *Benedict Option*, 9.

Introduction

Americans live openly rather than staying closeted, "living their sexual lives in shameful secrecy,"[4] and warns that separating sex from procreation led to the creation of brothels featuring robots.[5] While not all the popular Christian responses have been as dour or focused on sex, it is clear that more voices are needed. In this book, I want to introduce Thomas Merton to this conversation. It is geared towards a general audience, and as such, I provide background information about recent religious changes, the erosion of truth, and Merton's life and writings so that they can be better appreciated.

How can a monk who lived in the woods of rural Kentucky and died in 1968 credibly speak to our current and unprecedented times? Merton, while intentionally living apart from society, had a unique perspective on it. As such, he recognized and wrote about many of the trends we see today. We live in a consumer-driven society that promotes values that often impede us from being our true authentic selves. In addition, concerns about war, the fight for racial equality, and the struggle to know the truth are as relevant today as they were when Merton wrote about them.

I do not intend to draft Merton into the current culture war for a number of reasons. First, doing so distracts from the focus of this work and has the potential to be, in itself, divisive. Next, pulling Merton into specific battles of the modern culture war does a disservice to him and his legacy. It is unfair to take Merton or any other figure out of their own milieu and insert them into a modern scenario that would have been completely foreign to them. Of course, people can make informed guesses about how Merton would respond to a particular issue based on his writings and overall approach to related subjects. However, Merton was like all of us: a person of a particular time in history. Forcing him to speak directly about an issue he never contemplated is at best speculative and has the potential to be intellectually dishonest. Often when authors or speakers declare that they know how a notable figure from the past would respond to a new hot-button social issue the results are the opinions of those authors and speakers, selectively quoting the historical figure to justify their own position. Fortunately, Merton wrote extensively about issues that are still relevant today, and there is no need to engage him in this way.

In this book, I explore how Thomas Merton can provide a message of hope and a step towards unity in these chaotic times. Specifically, I look at Merton's writings and how he lived to provide a path for Christians working

---

4. Veith, *Post-Christian*, 107.
5. Veith, *Post-Christian*, 111.

to build God's kingdom in the world today. Therefore, in using Merton's life and writings as a model, one sees the importance of doing the following:

1. Don't retreat from the world—be an active part of it
2. Be a part of a faith community
3. Join in the suffering of others to work for change
4. Work for peace
5. Seek and affirm the truth wherever it is found

Despite all the challenges the world faced, Merton remained hopeful and believed that in this new era the unifying message of the gospel would continue to be preached. However, he believed that now "the purity of individual witness will take precedence over everything else."[6] There are no easy cures for the world's ills, but we cannot ignore them or fail to act simply because they seem to be insurmountable. Thomas Merton can provide a valuable model for each of us to be that individual witness to Christ in the world.

---

6. Merton, *Seeds of Destruction*, 198.

I

Where Are We and How Did We Get Here?

WE LIVE IN A post-Christian world. Thomas Merton recognized this during his lifetime and in 1962 defined it as being "a world in which Christian ideals and attitudes are relegated more and more to the minority."[1] He went on to declare that what often presents itself as a Christian society is "more purely and simply a materialistic neopaganism with a Christian veneer. And where the Christian veneer has been stripped off we see laid bare the awful vacuity of the mass mind, without morality, without identity, without compassion, without sense, and rapidly reverting to tribalism and superstition."[2] Since that time the American religious landscape has continued to change, with institutional Christianity declining in membership and influence. In this chapter, I survey the state of organized religion today and examine a handful of notable recent developments.

How Did We Get Here?

Part I. The Reformation

Our current religious environment is the culmination of changes that began centuries ago. Specifically, the Protestant Reformation and Enlightenment started a process of religious and philosophical fragmentation that

---

1. Merton, *Peace in the Post-Christian Era*, 72.
2. Merton, *Peace in the Post-Christian Era*, 72.

continues today. It is important to briefly examine these changes in order to better appreciate our current state of affairs. I have chosen to begin this inquiry with the Protestant Reformation, acknowledging that in addition to the real need for religious reform there were also a number of other factors, e.g., philosophical, social, economic, and political, that led to this watershed event.

While I and many others argue that the Reformation started a process of religious fragmentation that continues today, it is important to point out that the Reformation did not spring from a completely homogenous Christendom. Recognizing this fact helps put the current state of religiosity into a historical context. It is true that Roman Catholicism contains a comprehensive creed and code. However, history shows that what is taught as the "official" tenets of a particular faith often varies from the lived or everyday religion of the faithful. This is certainly true in the centuries leading up to the Reformation. There was no one single faith among the laity during this time. Instead, there was a spectrum ranging from various degrees of belief to unbelief.[3] There are many documented instances of Christians of this time questioning various aspects of the faith, including Christ's real presence in the Eucharist, the concept of purgatory, and the clerical and civil role of the clergy.[4] In addition, the role and veneration of saints sometimes elicited passionate responses. One medieval account describes an unnamed man who, incensed by the veneration of St. Aldhelm, lowered his breeches and broke wind in the direction of the saint's relics as they proceeded past him.[5]

The laity often incorporated a wide-ranging set of rival beliefs, including what was considered to be magic, in an effort to help make sense of and assert some kind of control over a world that was often violent and chaotic. These magical practices were not always meant to counter Catholic ones. Instead, they were often an amalgam of folk and Christian beliefs. For example, as historian Catherine Rider notes,

> charms that were recited over sick people to cure illnesses often invoked God and the saints; spells for love and other purposes might use consecrated substances such as the Eucharist; and one way of predicting the future was to use a book on lot-casting called

---

3. Arnold, *Belief and Unbelief in Medieval Europe*, 230.
4. Arnold, *Belief and Unbelief in Medieval Europe*, 217–18.
5. Arnold, *Belief and Unbelief in Medieval Europe*, 222.

the Lots of the Saints or Lots of the Apostles, which claimed to be based on the example set by the Apostles in the New Testament.[6]

This simultaneous belief in magic and Christianity persisted not just among the uneducated masses; it was also found in every social class, including the well-educated.[7] Texts about ritual magic were written by the educated for those who were both literate and affluent enough to purchase these books.[8] In addition, the belief in magic as a real force was given credibility when the church preached against its dangers and condemned those accused of being magicians. At times the state also gave credence to a belief in magic by outlawing its practice. For example, in 1441, the English government arrested a group, including scholars, clergy, and members of the palace court, for using magic.[9]

It is important to note that while folk practices like magic coexisted with Christianity there were also periods of organized opposition to the Catholic Church. There had always been those who disagreed with the church and who were labeled as "heretics." However, the Catholic Church in Europe faced its first theological and organized rival since the time of the late Roman Empire in Catharism.[10] The precise origins of this movement are unknown, but from the twelfth through the fourteenth century, tens of thousands of adherents, residing primarily in Southern France and Northern Italy, worked to build a rival church.[11] The Cathar Church was well organized and divided into dioceses, with bishops assigned to each of those areas. Each diocese also contained lay deacons and *perfecti* who acted as priests or ministers to the faithful. Other lay members were referred to as *credentes*.

The Cathars claimed to be the true Christian church, proclaiming that Catholicism was wrong doctrinally and had become corrupt. Their theology was built on older dualistic belief systems, e.g., Manichaeism, and Bogomilism, teaching that God and the devil were two eternal forces battling against each other—light versus dark.[12] The Cathar creation myth included a belief that the devil had snuck into heaven, recruiting souls to join him

6. Rider, *Magic and Religion in Medieval England*, 8.
7. Rider, *Magic and Religion in Medieval England*, 9.
8. Rider, *Magic and Religion in Medieval England*, 114.
9. Rider, *Magic and Religion in Medieval England*, 98.
10. Barber, *Cathars in Languedoc*, xi.
11. Weis, *Yellow Cross*, xxi.
12. Weis, *Yellow Cross*, xxi.

in exchange for earthly wealth. Once there, Satan created the human body. Based on this, Cathars believed things of the flesh were evil.[13] Partly influenced by this belief they rejected the virgin birth and the concept of transubstantiation. This disdain for the body can also be seen in their central sacrament—*consolamentum*. This was a rite done for one of the faithful on their deathbed. A *perfecti* would say a series of prayers, read from the gospel, and lay hands on the soon to be departed. They believed this process was vital to gain entry into heaven. Without it, the soul was doomed to be reincarnated, once again imprisoned in a human body.[14]

The growth of the Cathars posed a threat to Catholic authority. At first the Catholic hierarchy tried persuasion and debate in order to show them the "error of their ways." When that failed the Cathars were officially condemned in 1179 at the Third Lateran Council. After that did not bring about the desired Cathar conversion, Pope Innocent III proclaimed a crusade against the heretical group, leading to their eventual elimination.[15]

While the Christian faith may not have been completely homogenous before the Reformation, the path towards today's splintered religiosity started there. This is hardly a novel argument, with many scholars writing extensively to support that assertion.[16] The early reformers sought to usher in needed changes to the Catholic Church. Martin Luther's emphasis on the priesthood of all individual believers caused many Christians to look to themselves, rather than any institutional church, to be the ultimate arbiters of the meaning of Scripture, faith, and truth. As biographer Lyndal Roper writes, Luther elevated the role of the individual in matters of faith, giving ordinary Christians the "ability to decide who was preaching true Christian doctrine, rather than blindly accepting the word of the priest. Scripture was clear, Luther argued, and its meaning apparent to all."[17]

This authoritative turn to the self led to what theologian Mark C. Taylor describes as the privatization, deregulation, and decentralization of religious authority.[18] Taylor writes, "as religion was privatized and every believer became a priest, the centralized hierarchical authority of the church

---

13. Weis, *Yellow Cross*, 123–24.

14. Weis, *Yellow Cross*, 124.

15. Barber, *Cathars in Languedoc*, 4.

16. For example, see Brad S. Gregory's *The Unintended Reformation: How a Religious Revolution Secularized Society* and Mark C. Taylor's *After God*.

17. Roper, *Martin Luther*, 157.

18. Taylor, *After God*, 65.

broke down and authority was distributed among individual believers."[19] This rejection of the teaching authority of the Catholic Church resulted in the abandonment of a shared framework of knowledge.[20] For better or worse, this mostly monolithic faith had served as a common lens that all could use to view the world and evaluate issues of faith, morality, and life's ultimate questions. The Reformer's new reliance on *Solo Scriptura* did not lead to the Bible simply replacing Catholic teaching. Instead, it led to an array of scriptural interpretations and corresponding religious practices, all of which resulted in further segmentation. Historian Brad S. Gregory argues this very point:

> [T]he Reformation is the most important distant historical source for contemporary Western hyperpluralism with respect to truth claims about meaning, morality, values, priorities, and purpose. Despite the hopes and dreams of Reformation protagonists, the result of their distinctive appeal to scripture alone was not a set of clear mandates for reforming human life according to "the Gospel," but an undesired, open-ended range of rival truth claims about answers to the Life Questions.[21]

Part II. The Enlightenment

The Reformation implanted a belief in a growing number of Christians that they did not need a clerical system or church to discover the truth about Scripture and God. These trends gained momentum and, in some ways, changed trajectory in the mid-seventeenth century with the dawn of the Enlightenment. This wide-ranging intellectual movement was underpinned by a belief that old knowledge, be it from Greek philosophers or church teachings, should be treated with skepticism. Instead of relying on old belief systems there was an emphasis on modern thought and reason, thus earning the other moniker for this movement—the Age of Reason. The Enlightenment started in Western Europe and continued on into the nineteenth century.

It was within this context that the influence of organized religion began to wane. While most of the general public was largely oblivious to the

---

19. Taylor, *After God*, 65.
20. Gregory, *Unintended Reformation*, 326.
21. Gregory, *Unintended Reformation*, 369.

intellectual trends of the Enlightenment, the seeds of individual belief not reliant upon the mediation of a particular religion were further cultivated during this time. This trend would continue with the corresponding rise in literacy and the emerging middle class. This literate class of Western Europeans developed an intellectual curiosity and clamored for more knowledge. Commercial publishers sought to capitalize on this growing demand by producing a wide variety of works, many of which were not affiliated with or censored by any particular church.

During this time a new kind of religion emerged, heavily influenced by Enlightenment thought—Deism. It affirmed a belief that a benevolent and rational being created the universe. Deism also emphasized the use of reason, science, and knowledge derived through experience. It follows then that creation contains universal laws that can be known through the use of human reason. Based on this ethos Deism sought to remove any supernatural or miraculous elements, or any kind of private revelations that claimed to offer divine knowledge. Accordingly, prevailing Christian doctrines about the divinity of Jesus, the Trinity, the reliability of Scripture, etc. were disregarded. As philosopher Kerry S. Walters writes, Deists believed these long-held religious beliefs "violated ordinary human experience and were antithetical to the dictates of reason. Belief in them, they said, not only kept mankind in the shackles of superstition and ignorance but also insulted the majesty and dignity of God."[22]

Religion and Faith Today

In the last decade there has been a steady stream of research documenting changing attitudes about religion. The most thorough and noteworthy studies were produced by the Pew Research Center.[23] In 2007, and again in 2014, they explored the US religious landscape by taking over 35,000 phone surveys. In addition, Pew has done periodic updates, the most recent of which was published in October 2019. One of the key findings from all of this research is that the Christian portion of the United States is steadily declining, while the number of adults who do not identify with

---

22. Walters, *Revolutionary Deists*, 8.

23. The Pew Research Center describes itself as a nonpartisan "fact tank" that informs the public about the issues, attitudes, and trends shaping America and the world. It does not take policy positions. It conducts public-opinion polling, demographic research, media content analysis, and other empirical social science research.

any organized religion continues to rise. This trend is seen in every part of the country and every age bracket.[24] The percentage of adults who describe themselves as Christian dropped from 78.4 percent in 2007 to 65 percent in 2019. This decrease in Christian affiliation was primarily driven by a decline in Mainline Protestant and Catholic membership. While almost all Christian denominations saw a decrease, the number of nondenominational Evangelicals increased 1.5 percent between 2007 and 2014.[25] Many of these believers are affiliated with Protestant megachurches, which will be discussed later in the chapter.

Rise of the Nones

The continued growth of Nones, those people who select "None" when asked to identify their religious affiliation, has received a great deal of attention in the secular and religious press. The 2019 Pew update found that almost 26 percent of all Americans now consider themselves to be religiously unaffiliated.[26] This number is up from 16 percent in 2007.[27] To put that in perspective, the size of this group is now larger than all Mainline Protestant dominations combined.[28] This trend is likely to continue as the Millennial and younger generations get older, as these cohorts have a much lower rate of religious affiliation than older ones.[29]

Who Are the Nones?

There has been a great deal of research into what Nones actually believe. Most Nones, 68 percent, believe in God.[30] Many of these religiously unaffiliated, 37 percent, classify themselves as spiritual but not religious, believing that organized religions are, as one member of the survey described, "too concerned with money and power, too focused on rules and too involved

---

24. "America's Changing Religious Landscape," 3.
25. "America's Changing Religious Landscape," 21.
26. "In U.S. Decline of Christianity Continues," 3.
27. "America's Changing Religious Landscape," 4.
28. Drescher, *Choosing Our Religion*, 6.
29. "America's Changing Religious Landscape," 11.
30. "'Nones' on the Rise," 9.

in politics."[31] However, a third of Nones attend a worship service of some kind, usually in a church or other traditional house of worship, at least once a year.[32] Four percent of Nones are self-described atheists, with another 5 percent identifying as agnostic.[33] All of this quantitative data is invaluable in identifying trends. However, it can only provide a surface view. Luckily there is also a great deal of qualitative research available that provides a deeper glimpse into the lives of those Americans who have no religious affiliation.

In her book, *Choosing Our Religion: The Spiritual Lives of America's Nones*, Elizabeth Drescher argues that by choosing "None" one refuses "to participate in the normative system of religious identification, where labels suggest general agreement with beliefs, values, and practices that distinguish one religious institution from another."[34] In the past, terms like "pagan" or "heathen" were used to denigrate those who did not conform. Today however, the term "None" carries little of that negative weight.

Dresher conducted a number of focus groups with Nones to better understand what was most important to them. She found that many of them were opposed to religion because it "carries historical, ideological, and political baggage that is imagined as having traveled into contemporary life like a grumpy, argumentative uncle from the old country—stilted language, silly costumes, dated music, and an assumed (but by now largely evacuated) authority in tow."[35]

Many of the Nones Dresher met were raised in a religious faith. A number of former Mainline Protestants cited the boredom of repetitive teaching and emphasis on church attendance as reasons for leaving. Grounded in a moral and ethical tradition, these Nones were ready to "shed denominational identity like an old coat—maybe one they used to like a great deal, but which no longer fits into their adult lives."[36]

Those Nones who believe in God also saw themselves as actively creating spiritual meaning in their lives.[37] Dresher observes that our culture is infused with religious tropes and practices. It is understandable then

---

31. "'Nones' on the Rise," 10.
32. Drescher, *Choosing Our Religion*, 25.
33. "In U.S., Decline of Christianity Continues," 3.
34. Drescher, *Choosing Our Religion*, 30.
35. Drescher, *Choosing Our Religion*, 45.
36. Drescher, *Choosing Our Religion*, 69.
37. Drescher, *Choosing Our Religion*, 54.

that in the construction of their own religious identities many Nones use, sometimes idiosyncratically, material objects, traditions, and even parts of rituals found in established religious traditions.[38]

Theologian Linda A. Mercadante also did valuable qualitative research into the belief systems of Nones, focusing on those that profess some kind of spiritual belief. Based on interviews with hundreds of these individuals, she groups them into five categories: Dissenters, Casuals, Explorers, Seekers, and Immigrants. Dissenters are composed of three subgroups: Protesting Dissenters, Drifted Dissenters, and Conscientious Objector Dissenters. Protesting Dissenters stay away from organized religion for specific reasons, often related to some kind of negative personal experience. Mercadante found that this group only made up a small percentage of the Nones she interviewed. Drifted Dissenters do not have any particular axe to grind with religion, but drift away from organized religion and never go back, often justifying their decision by citing theological positions they reject. Finally, Conscientious Objector Dissenters express a long-held suspicion of religious institutions. These Nones concede that religion may be useful for some people, whom they often describe as being weak, but do not believe it is necessary in order to live a good or spiritual life.[39]

The next group of Nones, Casuals, approaches spirituality on an as-needed basis. They may occasionally read books, seek out a teacher, or attend religious services, but only when a specific need arises. These practices are primarily used as a way to relieve stress, gain better health, or for emotional support. Spirituality is not an organizing principle in the lives of Casuals. Instead, it is a tool to be used for a time and then dropped when no longer needed or of interest.[40]

Next, Explorers are not looking for a spiritual home. These Nones are driven by a kind of spiritual wanderlust, taking joy in the process of exploration and then "moving on as much from unsatisfied curiosity and the desire for novelty, as from disappointment."[41] Unlike many Casuals, Explorers are more aware of the theological differences between the various kinds of spiritualities they've sampled, and are unconcerned if not all of them fit together. They are happy to mix and match a variety of beliefs and spiritual practices that they've encountered during their spiritual tourism.

38. Drescher, *Choosing Our Religion*, 55.
39. Mercadante, *Belief without Borders,* 53.
40. Mercadante, *Belief without Borders,* 55–56.
41. Mercadante, *Belief without Borders,* 58.

Seekers, unlike Explorers, are looking for a spiritual home. Many of them still have a foot in one religious tradition while investigating others. These kinds of Nones were more common among Mercadante's interviewees who had a positive past religious experience and those who expressed a desire to belong to a group. Unlike the Explorers, Seekers are troubled by their inability to find a spiritual home.[42]

Finally Immigrants, the last group of Mercadante's spiritually oriented Nones, are individuals who have arrived at a new spiritual home. They were "usually newcomers 'trying on' the new environment, but were often not completely at home there."[43] Many of them reported difficulty adjusting to their new faith community. Mercadante speculates this difficulty is due to the fact that adopting a new spirituality requires commitment, constancy, and group loyalty. Those qualities are contrary to the values of independence, freedom, and nondogmatism that spiritually oriented Nones typically espouse.[44]

While Mercadante found characteristics that were unique to each of these subgroups of Nones she also identified several areas of agreement. All of them emphasized the importance of individual freedom in deciding one's own spiritual beliefs and practices. In addition, almost all of them were critical of theological views they associated with Western religious traditions. In a finding similar to that of Dresher, Mercadante's interviewees did not create new belief systems, but instead blended together various elements from a variety of existing traditions "resulting in an eclectic mixture which often produces an internally inconsistent schema. Yet although the pieces do not always fit together very well, many interviewees were either not aware of or not bothered by that fact."[45] Most of these Nones believe that all religions and spiritualities are essentially the same at their core, and are put off by claims that any one group has exclusive access to truth or salvation.[46] The number of people who identify as None is expected to keep growing.

---

42. Mercadante, *Belief without Borders*, 58–60.
43. Mercadante, *Belief without Borders*, 63.
44. Mercadante, *Belief without Borders*, 64.
45. Mercadante, *Belief without Borders*, 72.
46. Mercadante, *Belief without Borders*, 74–81.

The New Atheists

While the majority of Nones have some kind of spiritual belief there is a small but growing number who consider themselves to be atheists or agnostics. Self-described atheists are now 4 percent of the US population, an increase of 2 percent in the last ten years. Five percent of Americans identify as agnostic, up 2 percent from ten years ago.[47] In addition, a number of critics of organized religion and theism published bestselling books between 2004 and 2007, ushering in what became known as the New Atheist Movement. Sam Harris, Daniel Dennett, Richard Dawkins, and Christopher Hitchens became the most prominent members of this group of thinkers, ironically dubbed the Four Horsemen. While each takes a different approach in their critiques, they all agree that belief in God is intellectually indefensible. In addition, they all highlight the atrocities, both old and new, done in the name of religion.

Sam Harris published *The End of Faith: Religion, Terror and the Future of Reason* in the wake of 9/11. Harris is critical of all religions, writing that the idea that any one of them actually represents the infallible word of God "requires an encyclopedic ignorance of history, mythology, and art."[48] He also declares that the core beliefs of religious people are insane.[49] Speaking elsewhere, Harris states that religions have the power to unite people, but unfortunately that is done "generally by amplifying tribalism and spawning moralistic fears that would not otherwise exist."[50]

Harris directs his most vociferous criticism towards Islam. This is evident in statements such as "Islam, more than any other religion human beings have devised, has all the makings of a thoroughgoing cult of death,"[51] and the question "Is Islam compatible with a civil society? Is it possible to believe what you must believe to be a good Muslim, to have military and economic power, and to not pose an unconscionable threat to the civil society of others? I believe that the answer to this question is no."[52] Finally, Harris does not believe, based on feedback he received from formerly

---

47. "In U.S., Decline of Christianity Continues," 3.
48. Harris, *End of Faith*, 16.
49. Harris, *End of Faith*, 72.
50. Hitchens et al., *Four Horsemen*, 36.
51. Harris, *End of Faith*, 123.
52. Harris, *End of Faith*, 151.

religious people, that his work is just an academic exercise. Instead, it has the ability to win the war of ideas, faith versus disbelief.[53]

Daniel Dennett focuses on what he believes are the natural human impulses, both biological and psychological, that produced belief in God and subsequent religions. In his book, *Breaking the Spell: Religion as a Natural Phenomenon,* Dennett makes the case that this kind of belief is a product of the human evolutionary process. He argues that belief in God and shared faith promoted group cohesion, thus ensuring the cultural transmission of religion to subsequent generations. Religion is, therefore, "natural as opposed to *supernatural,* that is it is a human phenomenon composed of events, organisms, objects, structures, patterns, and the like that all obey laws of physics or biology and hence do not involve miracles."[54] Of these four thinkers Dennett has the most favorable attitude towards those who believe in God and he recognizes some of the positive contributions made by religion. He remains an unabashed atheist but believes "we should be concerned to preserve the good that organized religions can do" and has known people "whose lives would be desolate and friendless if it weren't for the nonjudgmental welcome they received in one religious organization or another."[55] In addition to the personal benefits that some derive from religious faith, Dennett believes institutional religions can also be a force for good, if changes are made. He writes "I am not in favor of ushering churches off the scene. I would rather assist in transforming these organizations into forms that are not caught in the trap of irrational—and necessarily insincere—allegiance to patent nonsense."[56]

The goal of Richard Dawkins's book *The God Delusion* is unambiguous. In the preface he writes "if this book works as I intend, religious readers who open it will be atheists when they put it down."[57] Like Dennett, Dawkins also points to the evolutionary process as a partial explanation for how belief in God emerged and survived. He traces how the human impulse to understand what appears to be the ordered design of the universe leads to the false belief that there was indeed a being who created it all. In addition, Dawkins dismisses intellectual arguments used over the centuries to support a belief in God, and affirms that the burden of proof

---

53. Hitchens et al., *Four Horsemen,* 85.
54. Dennett, *Breaking the Spell,* 25.
55. Dennett, *Breaking the Spell,* 31–32.
56. Dennett, *Breaking the Spell,* 32.
57. Dawkins, *God Delusion,* 28.

rests on believers, not on the nonbelievers: "the fact that orbiting teapots and tooth fairies are undisprovable is not felt, by any reasonable person, to be the kind of fact that settles any interesting argument. None of us feels an obligation to disprove any of the millions of far-fetched things that a fertile or facetious imagination might dream up."[58] Finally, Dawkins is adamant that children should not be indoctrinated into religions, and argues that they should not be labeled as being members of any particular faith, writing that "small children are too young to decide their views on the origins of the cosmos, or life and of morals. The very sound of the phrase 'Christian child' or 'Muslim child' should grate like fingernails on a blackboard."[59]

Finally, the last of the Four Horsemen, Christopher Hitchens is perhaps the best known of the New Atheists. Though he died in 2011, his writings continue to stir thought and debate. Hitchens is clearly opposed to theism of any sort, and he makes that case in his book *God Is Not Great: How Religion Poisons Everything*. He rails against the idea that people of the twenty-first century could still hold beliefs that were developed in prescientific times that lacked our modern understanding of the universe and our place in it. Religion that developed in these prehistoric times came "from the bawling and fearful infancy of our species, and is a babyish attempt to meet our inescapable demand for knowledge (as well as for comfort, reassurance, and other infantile needs)."[60] He argues that there are four main objections to religious faith: first, that it misrepresents the origins of the universe and humanity; second, because of this error, religious faith becomes inherently solipsistic; third, these faiths breed and perpetuate dangerous sexual repression; and fourth, religious belief is ultimately grounded in wishful thinking.[61]

Hitchens argues that many religious teachings are themselves immoral e.g., presenting a false picture of the world to the innocent and the credulous, the doctrines of blood sacrifice, the need for atonement, system of eternal rewards and punishments, and the imposition of impossible tasks and rules.[62] In addition, he contends that the number of competing religions begets a kind of tribalism that often leads to violence and intolerance.[63] In

58. Dawkins, *God Delusion*, 76.
59. Dawkins, *God Delusion*, 381.
60. Hitchens, *God Is Not Great*, 108.
61. Hitchens, *God Is Not Great*, 7.
62. Hitchens, *God Is Not Great*, 353.
63. Hitchens, *God Is Not Great*, 89.

fact Hitchens declares that totalitarianism is innate in all religions "because it has to want an absolute, unchallengeable, eternal authority . . . The Creator whose will can't be challenged. Our comments on his will are unimportant. His will is absolute, and applies after we're dead as well as before we're born. That is the origin of totalitarianism."[64]

Finally, Hitchens calls for a new Enlightenment. This time it will not be dependent upon a few influential thinkers but instead will emanate from average people. Now, thanks to the internet, nearly everyone has access to works of great literature that can help provide ways of framing life's ultimate questions, thus supplanting religious texts. In addition, this information revolution provides mass access to scientific information that can reorient previously religious world views. Finally, Hitchens hopes this movement will bring about "the divorce between the sexual life and fear, and the sexual life and disease, and the sexual life and tyranny . . . on the sole condition that we banish all religions from the discourse. And all this and more is, for the first time in our history, within the reach if not the grasp of everyone."[65]

Megachurches

Earlier in this chapter I noted that while Mainline Protestant church affiliation continues to decrease, nondenominational Evangelical church membership has increased. Many of these Christians are members of so-called megachurches. These churches earned their name partly because of their size, with congregations that average at least 2,000 attendees at weekend services. That figure is contrasted with the average churchgoer's congregation size of 400.[66]

The number of these churches has grown considerably in the last several decades. In 1970, there were around 50 megachurches,[67] and by 2015, that number had grown to 1,650.[68] The vast majority of these groups, 74 percent, are located in suburban areas. These churches are now so common that there is a megachurch within a ninety-minute drive of approximately 80 percent of the U.S. population.[69] Most of these congregations continue

64. Hitchens et al., *Four Horsemen*, 102.
65. Hitchens, *God Is Not Great*, 490.
66. "Religious Congregations in 21st Century America," 6.
67. Thumma and Travis, *Beyond Megachurch Myths*, 7.
68. "Megachurch Definition," para. 14.
69. Thumma and Travis, *Beyond Megachurch Myths*, 9.

to grow steadily, with a 2015 study finding that the median growth rate is 5 percent per year.[70]

I live in the Louisville, Kentucky area and it is home to one of the nation's largest megachurches—Southeast Christian Church. Throughout this section I will reference it to illustrate how the general characteristics of megachurches are embodied at a local level. In many ways the creation, growth, church facilities, and theology of Southeast Christian are representative of these types of congregations. Southeast Christian was founded in 1962, when fifty members of the South Louisville Christian Church felt a calling to start a new church in the city's growing eastern suburbs.[71] After three years, their first minister, Joe Rex Kearns, left to help start another church. After several experienced ministers turned down the offer to replace Kearns the church elders hired Bob Russell, a twenty-two-year-old recent graduate from Bible college.[72] Russell would go on to lead and grow Southeast Christian to become one of the largest churches in the United States.[73]

There is not a consensus on why these churches grew at such a rapid pace since the 1970s. However, in *Beyond Megachurch Myths: What We Can Learn from America's Largest Churches*, Scott Thumma and Dave Travis suggest it is partially attributable to Americans becoming more comfortable with large institutions during this time. In the last half of the twentieth century new hospitals, schools, and places to shop were built in order to accommodate larger crowds. As they put it, "after a week of working in a major corporation, shopping in a food warehouse and megamall, viewing movies at a multiplex theater, and having children who attend a regional high school, it seems incongruous that this family would feel comfortable in a forty-person church."[74]

The story of Southeast Christian's growth is remarkable. Three years after moving to the eastern suburbs the core group of fifty had expanded to 125 and was meeting in a supporter's basement. Anticipating more growth, they began construction on a church that could accommodate 400 worshipers.[75] Since that time the growing congregation prompted additional

70. Thumma and Bird, "Recent Shifts," 2.
71. Russell and Russell, *When God Builds a Church*, 3.
72. Russell and Russell, *When God Builds a Church*, 129.
73. "Outreach 100 List."
74. Thumma and Travis, *Beyond Megachurch Myths*, 15.
75. Russell and Russell, *When God Builds a Church*, 2.

moves into larger spaces. Finally, in 1998, they purchased 100 acres and launched one of the largest church capital campaigns in history, raising over 26 million dollars, to build their current church and campus.[76] Their growth continued with the creation of twelve satellite locations throughout the Louisville metropolitan area.

Another common trait of megachurches is their embrace of popular culture and the desire to cater to the comfort and needs of their congregants. For example, parking for the large services is well organized, with several attendants directing traffic like one would see at a concert or sporting event. Churches are spacious, with comfortable seating, and attendees have unobstructed views of the main stage and crisp video screens that provide close-up camera shots of the minister or other action occurring on stage. In addition, most of the music is a variety of Christian pop/rock. Lyrics for each song are displayed on video screens to encourage everyone to sing along. In these ways megachurches are able to appropriate familiar and desirable elements of popular culture, e.g., a version of popular music, without accepting all of its values.

Southeast Christian certainly embodies these traits. Police direct traffic to accommodate the crush of vehicles entering and exiting the campus. Once onsite, directions are clearly marked, with special parking spaces reserved close to the main building for first- and second-time visitors, as well as single parents. Cheerful volunteers greet congregants and visitors as they enter the large lobby. This area is well lit and resembles the interior of an upscale shopping mall, with a coffee shop, library, and bookstore located on its perimeter. When the service is about to begin, the lights dim, signaling it is time to take your seat in the multistoried main sanctuary. This large auditorium has seating for over 9,000, with clear views of the main stage, and resembles any other modern auditorium or fine arts center. It has no crosses, altar, or any other religious trappings found in most Mainline Protestant churches. A nine-piece band of talented musicians begins and ends each service with performances of Christian rock songs. Two camera operators move around the stage getting close-up shots of various musicians which are displayed on the four large video screens that flank each side of the stage. Several technicians mix and produce the audio and video, presenting a performance that is on par with any professional secular concert.

The megachurch phenomenon has prompted various reactions from the Christian community. There are those that are critical of these kinds of

---

76. Russell and Russell, *When God Builds a Church*, 131.

organizational and worship styles. *Christianity Today* succinctly summarized this backlash, writing that critics often rail "against theological superficiality, vapid worship music, and a seeker-sensitive, consumeristic ethos. Church growth strategies that emphasize upward movement in attendance figures over community cohesion and discipleship formation have also come in for criticism."[77] However, others see the proliferation of megachurches as the natural progression of American Protestantism, noting that Christian institutions in this country have always responded and adapted to changes in popular culture in order to remain relevant. For example, these groups can in many ways trace their origins to much older American churches. These megachurches employ elements that were introduced in several churches in the 1880s and 1890s. During that time, former theaters and auditoriums in large cities were repurposed as churches. Services held there were geared to appeal to the interests of the people at that time, with attention paid to the theatrical use of lighting, development of sound systems, and content tailored for cosmopolitan churchgoers.[78] Historian R. Laurence Moore makes the point that in order to remain relevant religion must be relatable to contemporary culture. He writes "after all, if religion is to be culturally central, it must learn to work with other things that are also central. Previously that might have been feudalism, kings, or Platonic philosophy. More recently it has been market capitalism responsive to consumers with spare time and a bit of money to spend."[79] Finally, some see the emergence of these churches as a paradigmatic shift within Christendom, enthusing that megachurches are:

> a second reformation that is transforming the way Christianity will be experienced in the new millennium . . . this reformation, unlike the one led by Martin Luther, is challenging not doctrine but the medium through which the message of Christianity is articulated. But what makes this reformation radical is that the hope of reforming existing denominational churches has largely been abandoned.[80]

Some megachurches have an affiliation with an established Protestant denomination, but research shows that these ties are often weak and these

---

77. "Megachurches," lines 5–7.
78. Kilde, *When Church Became Theater*, 215–20.
79. Moore, *Selling God*, 9.
80. Miller, *Reinventing American Protestantism*, 1.

congregations rarely rely upon them for resources or aid.[81] Southeast Christian, for example, is not affiliated with any particular denomination. Professor of Religion and Sociology Donald Miller argues that this lack of strong denominational affiliation and hierarchy helped attract Baby Boomers as it appealed to their countercultural impulses.[82]

Most megachurches encourage their members to be a part of small, interest-specific groups. Seventy-nine percent of megachurches consider these groups to be a central part of their organization's structure.[83] Small groups help foster a sense of community and allow members to meet other congregants with similar interests. Meetings and classes are designed for both prospective and seasoned members, covering a wide range of interests, including: studying aspects of the Christian faith, social justice issues, and individual self-improvement (this last one being the focus of many of these kinds of groups). Southeast Christian certainly exemplifies this trend by hosting a variety of groups, including those dedicated to Bible study, and support groups for veterans, families of the incarcerated, and those dealing with grief or facing adversity of some kind.

The growth of megachurch membership has been counter to the steady decline found in Mainline Christian denominations. However, there are signs that the trend of adults choosing to be Nones may also be impacting them. Recent survey data shows that over a five-year period the percentage of adult participants declined, both in the 18-to-34 and 35-to-49 age groups.[84] Many megachurches are actively working to combat the growing trend away from organized religion. One method is to appeal to those spiritually inclined Nones who aren't drawn to Catholic or Mainline Protestant congregations. In so doing these megachurches can respond to many of the reasons cited for turning away from organized faith and show why their congregations are different. The following sermon from Southeast Christian Church serves as a good example. On November 18, 2018, then-pastor Dave Stone delivered a sermon entitled "Moving from a Religion to a Relationship."[85] It begins with a forty-five-second PowerPoint type video presentation, featuring upbeat instrumental music and the following message:

81. Thumma and Bird, "Recent Shifts," 2.
82. Miller, *Reinventing American Protestantism*, 183.
83. Thumma and Bird, "Recent Shifts," 4.
84. Thumma and Bird, "Recent Shifts," 14.
85. Southeast Christian Church, "Moving from Religion to Relationship."

Where Are We and How Did We Get Here?

IN JESUS' TIME, PEOPLE WERE BURNED OUT ON LEGALISM
THEY LONGED FOR A FRESH ENCOUNTER WITH GOD
JESUS DIDN'T GIVE THEM A SET OF RULES
INSTEAD HE CALLED THEM TO A GREATER PURPOSE

Stone begins his sermon by pointing to the biblical figure of Nicodemus as an example of someone who went through a spiritual transformation, and moved from "laws and formality, to a personal relationship with the Messiah. He will move from a religion to a relationship. And I hope that if you have never gone on that journey yourself that you will take that same journey that Nicodemus has."[86] Stone then tells the congregants that "you need to know something about me. I don't like religion. And I know that might sound strange for a preacher to say, to tell you to be wary of something or to steer clear of something like religion. But listen, if you are put off by religion, I am right there with you."[87] He then goes on to say that religion can be a good thing if one uses a definition provided in James 1:27, which states that "Religion that God our Father accepts as pure and faultless is this: to look after orphans and widows in their distress." Stone continues, saying that in our culture today when one asks if a person is religious:

> they are rarely referring to how much time you spend volunteering with widows and orphans. And today when someone is said to be religious it's used as a description of some spiritual habit or some ritual or some practice. And because of that observers feel that that person has some level of spirituality. It really doesn't matter what they believe, it doesn't matter who they place their belief in. To our culture all that matters is the routine and the rituals that you practice. And that shows that you are religious. And maybe you've never heard anyone talk about the difference between a religion and a relationship.[88]

Stone goes on to say that religion isn't necessarily a bad thing, especially as defined above, but when it is reduced to a system of rituals "it can get sideways in a hurry."[89] He gives a personal example of a church he was once a part of that emphasized perfect attendance and encouraged its members to wear perfect attendance pins. Stone says "Maybe in your church it was a prayer you recited. Maybe it was kneeling. There's nothing

---

86. Southeast Christian Church, "Moving from Religion to Relationship," 4:54–5:10.
87. Southeast Christian Church, "Moving from Religion to Relationship," 5:18–5:36.
88. Southeast Christian Church, "Moving from Religion to Relationship," 5:58–7:01.
89. Southeast Christian Church, "Moving from Religion to Relationship," 7:22–7:25.

wrong with any of those things. There's nothing wrong with having perfect attendance. I think that's great. But when it becomes something that we flaunt, then it becomes something that we think."[90] His sermon then moves into the familiar theme of the importance of faith over acts as a way to be saved. He states that religion often stresses actions that one should take, whereas a spiritual relationship with Christ actually leads to salvation.

Stone directly addresses Nones, or those with similar inclinations, saying that there are "those of you who might be here, or are watching online or on TV, and you're skeptical of Christ and Christianity."[91] He then goes on to say that it's okay for someone to question their faith, just as Nicodemus did. Stone states Nicodemus eventually learned that:

> A relationship with Jesus will be much more fulfilling and freeing than a religion of rituals and rules that he was a part of. You see, Nicodemus and the other Pharisees, they fasted, they prayed, they gave ten percent back to the Lord. And don't get me wrong, those are important things, those are good things. But the Bible tells us that many of the religious leaders, they did it for the wrong reason. They did it to impress other people. They did it to enhance the way that other people viewed them.[92]

In showing the contrast between being religious and having a relationship with Christ, Stone says that for many being religious makes them feel "superior to others. They get caught up with empty rule-keeping. And the other just wants to get close to Christ."[93] Stone sums it all up by declaring that "a religion is filled with rules and restrictions. A relationship is filled with fulfillment and freedom."[94]

Finally, the growth and popularity of these megachurches is also influencing the worship style of some Mainline Christian congregations that are struggling to maintain their membership. There is a burgeoning church growth industry that holds seminars, sells books, and offers consulting services, all for the purpose of teaching established Protestant denominations how to emulate these growing megachurches. There are a variety of methods that some of these Mainline congregations employ to adapt and retool their worship services. One of these is the reframing of religious language,

---

90. Southeast Christian Church, "Moving from Religion to Relationship," 7:58–8:15.
91. Southeast Christian Church, "Moving from Religion to Relationship," 12:40–12:48.
92. Southeast Christian Church, "Moving from Religion to Relationship," 14:55–15:26.
93. Southeast Christian Church, "Moving from Religion to Relationship," 19:39–19:44.
94. Southeast Christian Church, "Moving from Religion to Relationship," 22:39–22:43.

symbols, and rituals. This is an effort to communicate the religious truths contained in the doctrine of these groups in a way that is more relatable and avoids the use of theological language.[95] Sociologist Stephen Ellingson found this process being used in a number of Lutheran churches in California. For example, some of these congregations reframed the word "sin" in a way that would be more relatable. One minister he interviewed said, "In my years of study I am persuaded that 'sin' is an important concept, but that sin doesn't work well. It isn't meaningful to people today. When you say 'sin,' no one is quite sure what it refers to. But alienation—separation, broken relationships—we get alienation. We all experience alienation. All humans are alienated."[96]

It will be interesting to see what else megachurches may do to blunt the growth of Nones, and what impact it will have on their congregations. It does, however, seem clear that the popularity of megachurches is not likely to wane, especially as they tailor their worship services and approach to those no longer interested in Mainline Christian denominations.

The Beliefs of Young People

In concluding this review of recent religious developments, it is important to examine the beliefs of young people. The move away from organized religion is seen in all age brackets. However, a deeper look into the data reveals that an even larger percentage of Nones are found in the Millennial and younger generations. Fully 35 percent of those surveyed do not consider themselves to be religiously affiliated, up 10 percent from 2007.[97] In addition, there is fascinating research that suggests that a majority of those young people who claim to be a part of a particular religious tradition do not actually espouse the beliefs of those faiths.

In the early 2000s, sociologists Christian Smith and Melinda Lundquist Denton conducted the largest and most comprehensive study of American teenage religion and spirituality ever done. As a part of their National Study of Youth and Religion they took telephone surveys of teenagers, ages thirteen to seventeen, and then perhaps more importantly, did in-depth interviews of these respondents in forty-five states.[98] Their survey

---

95. Ellingson, *Megachurch and the Mainline*, 82.
96. Ellingson, *Megachurch and the Mainline*, 82.
97. "America's Changing Religious Landscape," 70.
98. Smith and Denton, *Soul Searching*, 6.

was designed to incorporate a broad range of factors e.g., age, race, sex, socioeconomic status, rural, suburban, urban, region of country, and language spoken so as to appropriately represent teens nationwide.[99]

Eighty percent of their respondents said they believed in God.[100] Three-quarters of the surveyed teens were Christian, with 50 percent being Protestant and 25 percent Catholic.[101] Of those teens who professed to believe in God, 40 percent said they attended religious services once a week or more, with the same percent stating that they prayed daily or more often.[102] Nearly that same number of respondents were involved in a religious youth group at that time, with 68 percent stating they were then, or had previously been, involved in a such a group. In addition, 45 percent of teens had attended youth retreats, conferences, rallies, or congresses.[103] Not surprisingly, teenagers tended to connect to religion through organized group involvement.[104]

Sixteen percent of those surveyed did not consider themselves to be religious, although many of them prayed regularly and occasionally attended church services.[105] Twenty-nine percent reported that they believed only one religion was true, with 51 percent stating it was okay for people of one religious faith to also practice other ones.[106] Two-thirds of these teens said that a person did not need to be affiliated with a congregation in order to be religious or spiritual.[107] Many teenagers, across a variety of religious traditions, had a negative view of people they deemed to be too religious, and went to some lengths to distance themselves from them.[108] Only 2 to 3 percent would be described as spiritual seekers who were "self-directing and self-authenticating individuals pursuing an experimental and eclectic quest for personal spiritual meaning outside of historical religious traditions."[109]

---

99. Smith and Denton, *Soul Searching*, 6.
100. Smith and Denton, *Soul Searching*, 41.
101. Smith and Denton, *Soul Searching*, 31.
102. Smith and Denton, *Soul Searching*, 47.
103. Smith and Denton, *Soul Searching*, 54.
104. Smith and Denton, *Soul Searching*, 54.
105. Smith and Denton, *Soul Searching*, 31.
106. Smith and Denton, *Soul Searching*, 73–75.
107. Smith and Denton, *Soul Searching*, 76.
108. Smith and Denton, *Soul Searching*, 141.
109. Smith and Denton, *Soul Searching*, 79.

The majority of surveyed teenagers tende to follow the religious lead of their parents, with 3 out of 4 saying they considered their beliefs to be somewhat or very similar to their parents.[110] They "simply believe what they were raised to believe: they are merely following in their family's footsteps and that is perfectly fine with them."[111] Smith and Denton went on to conclude that for most of these teens, their inherited religious faith was less about a personal commitment to God and more of a way to avoid conflict with their parents.[112] As they write: "for most U.S. teenagers their claims to religion's importance notwithstanding, religion actually appears to operate much more as a taken-for-granted aspect of life, mostly situated in the background of everyday living, which becomes salient only under very specific conditions."[113] More about those kind of conditions in the following section.

Perhaps because of this taken-for-granted aspect of their faith, Smith and Denton found that the vast majority of their teen interviewees were "incredibly inarticulate about their faith, their religious beliefs and practices, and its meaning or place in their lives."[114] The researchers were careful to point out that they were not setting an unrealistic bar for these young people to hurdle. Instead, they argued that most religious teenagers either did not truly understand what their religious traditions professed or they did grasp it but simply did not believe it.[115] Smith and Denton summed up this point, writing: "nobody expects adolescents to be sophisticated theologians. But very few of the descriptions of personal beliefs offered by teenagers come close to representing marginally coherent accounts of the basic, important religious beliefs of their own faith traditions."[116]

In further analyzing their respondents' data Smith and Denton were able to identify some common beliefs that these young adults did actually espouse. They suggested that, regardless of whatever particular religion American teenagers professed to be a part of, there was instead an overriding de facto religion that was dominant amongst them. The researchers

---

110. Smith and Denton, *Soul Searching*, 34.
111. Smith and Denton, *Soul Searching*, 120.
112. Smith and Denton, *Soul Searching*, 124.
113. Smith and Denton, *Soul Searching*, 130.
114. Smith and Denton, *Soul Searching*, 131.
115. Smith and Denton, *Soul Searching*, 133.
116. Smith and Denton, *Soul Searching*, 137.

described this belief system as a kind of "Moralistic Therapeutic Deism." As such these teens professed the following beliefs:

1. A God exists who created and orders the world and watches over human life on earth.
2. God wants people to be good, nice, and fair to each other, as taught in the Bible and by most world religions.
3. The central goal of life is to be happy and to feel good about oneself.
4. God does not need to be particularly involved in one's life except when he is needed to resolve a problem.
5. Good people go to heaven when they die.[117]

None of these teens concisely profess this kind of faith. Instead, elements of this creed are assimilated, to various degrees, into elements of more traditional religious faiths. Moralistic Therapeutic Deism does not stand alone as a self-sustaining religion, but is instead parasitic, attaching itself "like an incubus to established historical religious traditions feeding on their doctrines and sensibilities, and expanding by mutating their theological substance to resemble its own distinctive image."[118]

In this kind of belief system, God exists, designed and created the world, and established a general moral order. This God is not especially involved in our daily lives and knows to keep a safe distance from us so as not to intrude in our lives. God is not demanding. Instead his role is to solve our problems and make us feel good, "In short God is something like a combination Divine Butler and Cosmic Therapist: he is always on call, takes care of any problems that arise, professionally helps his people to feel better about themselves, and does not become too personally involved in the process."[119]

Moralistic Therapeutic Deism holds that living a good life consists of being happy, kind, respectful to others, working on self-improvement, and being successful, "it is about attaining subjective well-being, being able to resolve problems, and getting along amiably with other people."[120] This emphasis on feeling good and being nice to others works to ease any potential tension with those who hold different beliefs. This kind of faith doesn't call

117. Smith and Denton, *Soul Searching*, 162.
118. Smith and Denton, *Soul Searching*, 166.
119. Smith and Denton, *Soul Searching*, 165.
120. Smith and Denton, *Soul Searching*, 164.

for sacrifice, or guide people to be the kind of individuals God wants them to be. It is instead a means of meeting one's own needs.

According to Denton and Smith, religious faith, and Christianity in particular, are not being secularized. Instead, they argue established religions are being colonized and supplanted by the tenets of Moralistic Therapeutic Deism and are degenerating into pathetic versions of themselves.[121] Finally, they suspect that this kind of religious thinking is not likely to be confined to just young people. Instead, they warn that "it may be the new mainstream American religious faith for our culturally post-Christian, individualistic, mass consumer, capitalist society."[122]

Conclusion

We continue to live in a post-Christian world, just as Merton observed decades ago. Since that time there have been a number of changes, not only in declining membership in Mainline Protestant and Catholic congregations, but also with the kind of faith espoused by many young members of these groups. In addition, the turn away from organized religion has continued with more and more people identifying as Nones. Megachurches, however, have managed to grow steadily, largely by incorporating elements of popular culture and often tailoring their message to appeal to those disinterested in other forms of Christianity or organized religion. All of these religious changes are occurring in a broader secular society that is increasingly divided, in which the very concept of truth is under assault. The next chapter examines that phenomenon.

---

121. Smith and Denton, *Soul Searching*, 171.
122. Smith and Denton, *Soul Searching*, 262.

2

Post-Truth

IN ADDITION TO LIVING in a post-Christian world, we also find ourselves in a post-truth one. The "truth" of a thing is often less important than one's opinions about it. This phenomenon got widespread attention in late 2016 when the Oxford Dictionary named "post-truth" as its word of the year. It defines "post-truth" as "relating to or denoting circumstances in which objective facts are less influential in shaping public opinion than appeals to emotion and personal belief."[1] This concept was introduced into popular culture over a decade earlier by comedian Stephen Colbert. In October 2005, appearing as his satirical conservative pundit character, Colbert introduced the word "truthiness." After telling his audience that he was a straight shooter and would always speak to them in simple, plain English, he explained the concept of "truthiness":

> Now I'm sure some of the "word police," the "wordinistas" over at Webster's, are gonna say, "Hey, that's not a word!" Well, anybody who knows me knows that I'm no fan of dictionaries or reference books. They're elitist. Constantly telling us what is or isn't true. Or what did or didn't happen. Who's Britannica to tell me the Panama Canal was finished in 1914? If I wanna say it happened in 1941, that's my right. I don't trust books—they're all fact, no heart . . . Face it, folks, we are a divided nation . . . divided between those who think with their head and those who know with their heart . . . Because that's where the truth comes from, ladies and gentlemen—the gut.[2]

1. McIntyre, *Post-Truth*, 14.
2. Andersen, *Fantasyland*, 3.

Whether we call it post-truth or truthiness, both terms point to the diminishing importance of facts and primacy of opinion, all at the cost of ever getting at the truth. Why is post-truth so prominent today? As I will discuss, there are some historic precursors for this kind of blurring of fact and opinion. However, the current prevalence of post-truth is attributable to a biological tendency to seek out facts that corroborate our existing beliefs that has been turbocharged by a transformed media landscape and new ways that people receive and consume information.

One of the psychological factors that predisposes us to keep believing what we've always thought to be true, regardless of the facts, is confirmation bias—a predisposition to favor information that supports our current beliefs rather than accept that we are wrong. As philosopher Lee McIntyre succinctly puts it, "it just feels better for us to think that we are smart, well-informed, capable people than that we are not."[3] This is because holding two ideas or beliefs that are inconsistent creates a state of tension or cognitive dissonance.[4] This dissonance makes us feel bad, producing a range of emotions from minor pangs of anxiety to debilitating grief. In response to this feeling, a hardwired physiological mechanism "creates self-justification and protects our certainties, self-esteem and tribal affiliations."[5] Towards that end we will criticize, distort, or simply ignore new information in order to maintain or even strengthen our existing beliefs.[6] For example, researchers found that when political partisans were presented with evidence that one of their political beliefs was objectively wrong, subjects would reject that evidence, steadfastly holding onto their mistaken views. In addition, another study found that the reasoning areas of the brain shut down when subjects were presented with dissonant information. This provides scientific support for the observable fact that changing someone's mind can be an extraordinarily difficult task.[7]

Research also suggests that the tendency of one group to be dismissive of, or hostile towards, a rival may be ingrained in human behavior. Evolutionary psychologists argue that this sense of tribalism played a key role in survival over countless generations. Working closely with members of one's own tribe to achieve the common good and ensure survival promoted

3. McIntyre, *Post-Truth*, 39.
4. Tavris and Aronson, *Mistakes Were Made*, 17.
5. Tavris and Aronson, *Mistakes Were Made*, 12.
6. Tavris and Aronson, *Mistakes Were Made*, 24.
7. Tavris and Aronson, *Mistakes Were Made*, 27.

group cohesion. Thus, the groups that prospered were those whose members substantially thought the same way and were leery of any dissenting voices. When we become anxious, angry, or threatened, our blind spots are automatically triggered, producing thoughts that other groups aren't as smart, reasonable, or trustworthy as our own.[8]

Post-truth may have entered the cultural mainstream in the last several years, but it does have some historical precedents. In their book, *Truth Decay: An Initial Exploration of the Diminishing Role of Facts and Analysis in American Public Life*, Jennifer Kavanagh and Michael D. Rich show how changes in the media in three different eras clouded the understanding of truth. First, the 1880s and 1890s saw the birth of yellow journalism, and with it the blurring of opinion and facts. The newspaper market was dominated by William Hearst and Joseph Pulitzer, whose desire for subscribers and profits encouraged each to print sensationalized and often embellished stories about crime and political intrigue. Yellow journalism was an early form of "fake news" in which false or misleading stories were used to appeal to readers and sell papers.[9] During this time there was a rapid increase in the reach and circulation of mass-produced newspapers and monthly journals. Between 1890 and 1905, the circulation of monthly journals increased from 18 million to 64 million.[10]

Second, one can also see a blurring between facts and opinions in the 1920s and 1930s. Tabloid journalism, also known then as "jazz journalism," arose during this time and promoted sensationalized and even fabricated stories of sex and violence that were intended to attract readers. This type of "news" grew in popularity and prompted more established publications to modify their content in an effort to retain readership. Thus, such non-news content like advice columns, short stories, and editorials was added. As Kavanagh and Rich describe it, "this shift in content increased the volume of opinion and anecdote, often at the expense of facts and it resembles changes observed more recently among conventional media outlets struggling to compete with newer web-based publications that offer less news but are more appealing."[11] In addition, during this time radio became an important force in the media market. In 1930, approximately 40 percent of households in the United States had radios. That number ballooned to 85

---

8. Tavris and Aronson, *Mistakes Were Made*, 82.
9. Kavanagh and Rich, *Truth Decay*, 79.
10. Kavanagh and Rich, *Truth Decay*, 79.
11. Kavanagh and Rich, *Truth Decay*, 86.

percent by the end of the decade.[12] Radio programs included news broadcasts, comedies, dramas, and religious and political shows. Not only did radio further democratize access to information, it also gave birth to radio personalities who developed vast and loyal followings. As Kavanagh and Rich point out, radio "facilitated the spread of opinion and commentary to a wide audience and made it increasingly difficult to distinguish fact from opinion. It was difficult to assess the trustworthiness of any individual radio host and even more difficult for listeners to 'fact check' information they heard on a radio program."[13]

Finally, "New Journalism," a reporting style that relies on subjective perspective and emphasizes personal experience and beliefs over objective facts, arose in the 1960s and early 1970s.[14] This was seen not only in established print journalism but also in the burgeoning television news industry. By 1966, 90 percent of Americans owned a television. Thus, this trend towards subjectivity in the news was spread to more Americans than any media ever had before this time.[15] In each of these periods the blurring of fact and opinion was fueled by changes in how media was distributed and consumed. This would be a precursor to the paradigmatic shift created by 24-hour cable news, the internet, and social media.

The internet, and social media in particular, can now bring us an endless supply of information; a gushing stream of news and opinion sluiced out to our phones, tablets, watches, and computers. A recent Pew poll shows that the vast majority of American adults get their news from social media.[16] News is now distributed and spread instantaneously, often containing a mix of fact and opinion. In addition, much of this information does not go through traditional media filters, e.g., editorial fact checking. This often results in the spread of incomplete, inaccurate, and outright false information.

Consuming news online and through social media allows us to create our own echo chambers where we only receive content that generally agrees with our worldview. This in turn causes us to become even more entrenched in our thinking. This is both an active and passive process. One actively participates by following a particular media personality, "sharing"

12. Kavanagh and Rich, *Truth Decay*, 86.
13. Kavanagh and Rich, *Truth Decay*, 87.
14. Kavanagh and Rich, *Truth Decay*, 95.
15. Kavanagh and Rich, *Truth* Decay 96.
16. McIntyre, *Post-Truth*, 79.

and "liking" content, or reading certain webpages. However, there is also a passive component. The filters and algorithms embedded in social media platforms and web search engines, as well as news aggregators e.g., Yahoo, Google, and iPhone News apps, are all skewed to deliver news and information-based content that is similar to what we've engaged with in the past.[17]

These disruptive technological changes in how information is targeted and delivered to consumers comes on the heels of significant changes to traditional media. Some of these shifts predate the emergence of the internet. In 1980, CNN became the world's first 24-hour cable news network. Thus, the traditional morning and evening news cycles gave way to a 24-hour one. In order to fill all of that time a great deal of commentary on the news was added, with this mix of reporting and commentary blurring the line between fact and opinion. CNN's success attracted more media organizations to the market who were dedicated to twenty-four hours of news. In the past, the news departments for major networks had not been profit centers. Now, however, these stand-alone news networks had to focus on profitability. These economic concerns encouraged media organizations to tailor their coverage to audience biases, "essentially providing the types of news stories that people want and agree with, rather than focusing on providing high-quality and objective news coverage."[18]

Finally, a discussion of post-truth and the media landscape would be incomplete without touching upon the rise of overtly partisan programing. The Rush Limbaugh radio program debuted in 1988 and quickly became a conservative media juggernaut, being syndicated to hundreds of radio stations and heard by tens of millions of people every afternoon.[19] Based on this success other conservative and liberal radio and TV talk programs followed, culminating in the creation of the conservative Fox News Network. Debuting in 1996, its stated objective was to offer "Fair and Balanced" reporting of the news, providing a conservative counter to what it believed was a prevalent liberal media bias.

Fox has been wildly successful and spawned an even further partisanation of cable news, with MSNBC staking out a deliberately progressive position. Since the 2016 Presidential election two starkly different worlds are presented on a nightly basis. MSNBC and CNN (on the left), and Fox (on the right) turn their nightly programing over to commentators. Each

17. Kavanagh and Rich, *Truth Decay,* 147.
18. Kavanagh and Rich, *Truth Decay,* 129.
19. McPhate and Sisario, "4 More Years."

selectively presents curated facts to describe a very particular kind of world. All of this is delivered by head-shaking hosts who marvel at how those on the other side of the political divide could be so wrong.

The Death of Expertise

Within this post-truth environment there is also a growing contempt for the knowledge held by experts. In his book, *The Death of Expertise: The Campaign against Established Knowledge and Why It Matters*, Tom Nichols argues that during this time of unprecedented access to knowledge Americans are increasingly resistant to actually learning anything. There has always been a tendency to root for the average Jane or Joe who uses common sense or "folk wisdom" to show that they actually know more about a particular subject than, or can outperform, some overeducated egghead.[20] However, this intensified disregard of expert opinions is new and not just found in groups who have lower levels of formal education. As will soon be shown, there are instances where those with higher educations are equally dismissive of expert knowledge.

This rejection of expertise should not be confused with healthy intellectual skepticism. Instead, Nichols argues that there is growing hostility towards expert views or established knowledge, along with the belief that "every opinion on any matter is as good as every other."[21] This is fueled in large part by the boundless information available on the internet. However, as Nichols points out, "knowing things is not the same as understanding them. Comprehension is not the same thing as analysis. Expertise is not a parlor game played with factoids."[22] All of this is leading to the death of expertise itself. He sums up his concerns, writing, "I fear we are witnessing the death of the ideal of expertise itself, a Google-fueled, Wikipedia-based, blog-sodden collapse of any division between professionals and laypeople, students and teachers, knowers and wonderers—in other words, between those with any achievement in an area and those with none at all."[23] This trend can be seen in a number of areas, but one of the most noteworthy is the increasing distrust of science, displayed in the pre-COVID-19 anti-vaccine movement.

20. Nichols, *Death of Expertise*, 38.
21. Nichols, *Death of Expertise*, 20.
22. Nichols, *Death of Expertise*, 37.
23. Nichols, *Death of Expertise*, 2.

There have always been vaccine skeptics, starting in 1796 with people who opposed the smallpox vaccine.[24] However, until very recently it was widely accepted that the benefits of vaccines outweighed the risks.[25] That started to change in 1982 with the airing of a NBC documentary. "DPT: Vaccine Roulette" focused on a number of English parents that believed a vaccine to prevent lung disease caused seizures in young children. While many medical experts at the time objected to inaccuracies in the program, concerned viewers formed anti-vaccination groups.[26] This anti-vax movement grew considerably in 1998 after Andrew Wakefieled, a British gastroenterologist, published a study in *Lancet* that linked the MMR vaccine with autism. Wakefield's research was subsequently discredited, but not before it gained a great deal of mainstream attention.

A number of celebrities joined the anti-vax cause, amplifying its message. Many of them pointed to Wakefield's study when speaking out against what they believed to be the danger of vaccines. Most notably, actress Jenny McCarthy became the public face of the anti-vaccine movement in the early 2000s as she explored traditional and alternative treatments for her autistic son. Her appearance on *The Oprah Winfrey Show* clearly illustrates a post-truth lack of respect for expert knowledge. McCarthy declared she was qualified to authoritatively speak about the link between vaccines and autism because of all the internet research she had done. She proudly proclaimed "the University of Google is where I got my degree from!"[27]

This privileging of personal opinions, based on online "research," over those of experts is not just confined to celebrities. As Dr. Paul A. Offitt, an infectious disease expert at Children's Hospital of Philadelphia describes it, "science has become just another voice in the room. It has lost its platform. Now, you simply declare your own truth."[28] This trend is spreading throughout the country, in both red and blue states.[29] In some cases it is more prevalent in urban areas, among those with a higher education, than rural ones where the population tends to be less educated. For example, the San Francisco suburbs of Marin County had lower childhood vaccination rates compared to rural areas. Professor Tom Nichols declares, "while these

---

24. Hoffman, "How Anti-Vaccine Sentiment Took Hold," para. 23.
25. Kavanagh and Rich, *Truth Decay*, 39.
26. Hoffman, "How Anti-Vaccine Sentiment Took Hold," para. 23.
27. Andersen, *Fantasyland*, 7.
28. Hoffman, "How Anti-Vaccine Sentiment Took Hold," para. 6.
29. Kavanagh and Rich, *Truth Decay*, 53.

mothers and fathers are not doctors, they are educated enough to believe they have the background to challenge established medical science. Thus, in a counterintuitive irony, educated parents are actually making worse decisions than those with far less schooling."[30]

And Then There's Bullshit

Philosopher Harry Frankfurt describes another pervasive trend that further shows this growing apathy towards the truth—bullshit. In his best-selling book, *On Bullshit,* Frankfurt observes that bullshit is ubiquitous in our culture and contributed to by everyone. Despite its existence being taken for granted, there has been no real effort to fully understand it. Frankfurt applies philosophical analysis to begin the development of a theoretical understanding of bullshit.[31]

What is bullshit? It is best understood when compared to a lie. In order to tell a lie the liar must know and care about what is true. In lying, one inserts a deliberate falsehood, at a specific time, into a set or system of beliefs, in order to avoid the consequences of having that point occupied by the truth. In order to create an effective lie one must create a falsehood that corresponds to that truth. The bullshitter, on the other hand, does not have the same commitment to know the truth as a liar. A person who bullshits has much more freedom since he or she does not have to stake out a particular position that is within the orbit of the truth. The bullshitter is not limited to inserting a certain falsehood at a specific point and is thus not constrained by the truths surrounding it.[32] Frankfurt writes that the bullshitter employs more creativity than analysis, "it is more expansive and independent, with more color and imaginative play. This is less a matter of craft than of art. Hence the familiar notion of a 'bullshit artist.'"[33] The bullshitter's prime motivation is to bluff his or her way through a particular situation. As Frankfurt writes, the bullshitter "is neither on the side of the true nor on the side of the false. His eye is not on the facts at all, as the eyes of the honest man and of the liar are, except insofar as they may be pertinent to his interest in getting away with what he says. He does not care whether the things he says describe reality correctly. He just picks them

---

30. Nichols, *Death of Expertise,* 20.
31. Frankfurt, *On Bullshit,* 1.
32. Frankfurt, *On Bullshit,* 50.
33. Frankfurt, *On Bullshit,* 50.

out, or makes them up, to suit his purpose."[34] Bullshitters, then, are frauds who attempt to manipulate the opinions and attitudes of those to whom they communicate. They are far more interested in successfully manipulating others and are indifferent to whether what they say is true or false.[35]

Bullshit has always existed in American society, and politics in particular. Politicians have a long history of telling lies and using bullshit in order to craft a particular narrative or to avoid answering uncomfortable questions. However, the 2016 presidential election ushered in the Golden Age of political bullshit, with President Trump's own spokesperson saying, with a straight face, that the president used "alternative facts."

Post-Truth as a Part of the American Ethos

This post-truth environment is not just an American phenomenon. The Brexit campaign in Great Britain famously featured many false claims in support of their position to leave the European Union. For example, hundreds of buses were covered with pro-Brexit statements, including a false statistic that the United Kingdom was sending 350 million euros a week to the European Union.[36] However, in his book, *Fantasyland: How America Went Haywire: A 500-Year History,* Kurt Andersen argues that the very impulses that spawned the United States and helped it grow and flourish may make us uniquely prone to post-truth. America was founded in large part by those who wanted to practice religion as they saw fit, with a Protestant emphasis on the individual believer being the ultimate arbiter of truth.[37] It was also founded by those who wanted to reinvent themselves in a new land and put the Enlightenment ideals of intellectual freedom into practice, with every individual free to believe whatever they wished.[38] Finally, a history of America includes a long line of dreamers, idealists, and even hucksters helping to create a spirit of American Exceptionalism and the absolute right of Manifest Destiny. Andersen proposes that our current post-truth society is due in large part to the fact that we're Americans, "because being American means we can believe any damn thing we want and that our beliefs are equal or superior to anyone else's, experts be damned.

34. Frankfurt, *On Bullshit*, 56.
35. Frankfurt, *On Truth*, 3–4.
36. McIntyre, *Post-Truth*, 15.
37. Andersen, *Fantasyland*, 17.
38. Andersen, *Fantasyland*, 5.

Once people commit to that approach, the world turns inside out, and no cause-and-effect connection is fixed. The credible becomes incredible and the incredible credible."[39]

Postmodernism

Finally, no discussion of post-truth would be complete without examining the influence of the postmodernist movement. Postmodernism sprang from academic literary criticism in the 1980s that posited one must deconstruct a text and examine it as a function of the political, social, historical, and cultural assumptions in which it was created in order to fully understand it.[40] This theorizing soon spread to other academic disciplines. Postmodernists believed that in creating these texts and theories people unavoidably brought their own values, prejudices, etc. into the mix. Therefore, the idea that there was a right or wrong meaning of a particular text was thrown into question.[41] As Professor Lee McIntyre puts it, "the postmodernist approach is one in which everything is questioned and little is taken at face value. There is no right answer, only narrative."[42] It follows then that any kind of truth claims are just the reflection of the individual ideology of the person making them.[43] Postmodernists assert that since all truth is subjective and all knowledge culturally bound to a particular narrative, those in a position of authority who proclaim something to be universally true are in reality exerting their power in "an attempt to force all people everywhere to adopt the same truth and values of the promoter (with the ultimate aim of enslavement and oppression.)"[44] While it is true that postmodernism sprang from liberal academics, these same guiding principles have been adopted by some conservatives who doubt various elements of science, e.g., evolution and climate change. People on both sides of the political divide now voice their doubts about truth and objectivity, and accuse those in power of distorting or fabricating facts to further their own political ends.[45]

---

39. Andersen, *Fantasyland*, 7.
40. McIntyre, *Post-Truth*, 102.
41. McIntyre, *Post-Truth*, 103.
42. McIntyre, *Post-Truth*, 103.
43. McIntyre, *Post-Truth*, 103.
44. Wilber, *Trump and a Post-Truth World*, 6.
45. McIntyre, *Post-Truth*, 108.

This notion that postmodernism led to our current state of post-truth is not universally accepted. However, it certainly seems to have fostered an environment in which post-truth could thrive. Philosopher Daniel Dennett, who was mentioned in the last chapter, convincingly makes the connection between postmodernism and post-truth. In discussing his concerns about post-truth today he states, "the real danger that's facing us is we've lost respect for truth and facts . . . it doesn't matter how good your facts are, somebody else can spread the rumor that you're fake news. We're entering a period of epistemological murk and uncertainty that we've not experienced since the middle ages."[46] He goes on to directly blame postmodernism for the waning importance of truth in our culture, "sometimes, views can have terrifying consequences that might actually come true. I think what the postmodernists did was truly evil. They are responsible for the intellectual fad that made it respectable to be cynical about truth and facts."[47] This descent into post-truth is not likely to change anytime soon. That is why it is important for people to be aware of it and do everything possible to seek out and affirm the truth. Thomas Merton can serve as a valuable role model in this effort and can also help us take on other challenges found in our post-Christian and post-truth world.

---

46. Cadwalladr, "Daniel Dennett," para. 5.
47. Cadwalladr, "Daniel Dennett," para. 9.

3

Why Merton?

It would be easy for someone unfamiliar with Thomas Merton to dismiss him as being irrelevant to Christians today. What can we learn about our world from a monk who lived most of his adult life in the woods of Kentucky and died over a half century ago? In the rest of this book I hope to show that the answer to that is—plenty! People of all faiths are drawn to Merton's work for its insights about God and the human condition. Furthermore, a close look at his life reveals his humanity, his triumphs, and his disappointments, and makes him an eminently relatable figure. In this chapter I introduce Thomas Merton and begin to show why he is indeed a compelling and relevant model for Christians today.

Thomas Merton is one of the most influential Catholic writers of the twentieth century. This is due not only to the quality of his work but also his prodigious output, having written over 60 books, dozens of articles and essays, as well as poetry. This productivity is even more impressive when one considers that for most of Merton's life as a monk his time to write competed with the other regimented obligations of his daily life. He first came to prominence in 1948 with the publication of his autobiography, with new generations of readers discovering his wisdom and insights about contemplation and ways to better know God. In fact, it has been argued that his extensive writings about contemplation helped modernize the practice in the Christian tradition.[1]

While Merton's earlier writings focused on the interior experience of knowing God, in the last years of his life he wrote more about the exterior

---

1. Park, *Thomas Merton's Encounter*, 51–52.

world and the problems in it. These writings helped shape the conversation about a host of spiritual and social issues, including racism, war, the proliferation of nuclear weapons, and ways our consumeristic society distracts and prevents us from pursuing those things that can provide true happiness and fulfillment. Finally, during this period Merton wrote about his exploration of Zen and Buddhism and helped establish an important bridge between Western Christianity and Eastern thought.

Many readers report that after discovering Merton they feel a kind of kinship with him. One reason many cite is his ability to grasp and convey profound insights about the human experience and God. As one biographer writes:

> He had the ability to articulate, often with brilliance and astounding perceptiveness, the vagaries of the human condition: hope vying with despair, love with hatred, communion with alienation. He could reach deep into the human heart and surface questions for his readers that, till they read him, lay hidden and unasked, struggling for expression. Unique synthesizer that he was, he could put things together that no one had seen as one before. He knew how to raise to a new level of understanding people's perception of God and prayer and human life. He was able to show that life was for the living in that in this living we find God and self and meaning and purpose.[2]

In addition, Merton was able to assimilate information and identify trends earlier than other writers or social critics. One of his friends described it this way:

> He was as capacious a mind as I've ever encountered. He took everything in, tied it together, and somehow it came out always in an orderly way. It was a good thing that he chose the essay as his way of dealing with the world. He was a monk and he just had little hunks of time to write. But in two or three hours it's amazing the cogent gems he could turn out. He was an exceptionally sensitive man, as well as an exceptionally religious man. The race situation, the bomb—he saw the consequences clearly and early, and from a place so far out of the mainstream. He was years ahead of almost everybody in his concern that the machines were going to take over—the whole business of dehumanization. And he was quite right.[3]

2. Shannon, *Silent Lamp*, 5–6.
3. Wilkes, *Merton*, 88.

Why Merton?

No one familiar with Merton's life story would confuse him for being any kind of, to use one of his own terms, pseudoangel. He never claimed to be perfect, and was thoroughly human, filled with the same conflicting instincts that live in all of us. Merton's life as a cloistered monk did not shield him from conflict, pettiness, worry, or self-doubt. For example, many biographers point to the fact that Merton was restless. Once he attained one thing, he wanted another. As one friend of his puts it:

> He loved people, he really loved people. But at the same time as he loved them he wanted his distance from them. People would often say to me that they found it odd, if not slightly scandalous, that a monk could share a few beers with you, just call from the monastery and arrange for a picnic, and yet I think this was a lifeline for him. He didn't want the secular life but he needed the reassurance that came by being with people. He was a fusser and a complainer to tell you the truth and when you read his journals you see that when he is here he wants to be there: if he's in the hermitage, he needs to get out; if he is following one diet maybe he should be really following another. He was, with all these contradictions, just plain human.[4]

While Merton's reputation for profundity draws people to his writings, I contend it is his ordinary humanness that makes him so appealing. In his personal writings, his journals and innumerable letters, we are able to glimpse Merton the person. This allows us to move beyond the categories of "monk" and "writer" to get to know Thomas Merton the man. What we find in these writings is a mix of the mundane and the sublime. Profound insights about God's grace in the world are mixed with complaints about life that are recognizable to everyone, both inside and outside the monastery walls. Merton chronicles his struggles with authority, the annoyance of living and working with others, and the inevitable aches and pains that accompany middle age. Merton was, just like the rest of us, a flawed work in progress.

Merton—A Brief Biography

There are a number of excellent Merton biographies that thoroughly explore every aspect of his life. The following narrative is intended for those returning to Merton after a long break or meeting him for the first time.

---

4. Higgins, *Thomas Merton*, 73–74.

Childhood

Thomas Merton was born during a snowstorm in Prades, France on January 31, 1915. His parents had met in 1911, while enrolled as art students at the Tudor-Hart Academy in Paris. His father, Owen, was an artist and musician, and his mother, Ruth, was a dancer and painter.[5] Within a year of Thomas's birth the family had moved to America to be near Ruth's family and so that Owen could avoid conscription into the Great War. Ruth's parents, Samuel "Pop" and Martha "Bonnemaman" Jenkins, would play an important role in Merton's upbringing. Owen and Ruth led a largely hand-to-mouth existence while living in America. They had vowed not to accept any money from Ruth's parents, except when they needed medicine for young Thomas.[6] Owen was always able to keep the family afloat financially, if just barely, by working a series of odd jobs, including church organist, playing piano at a local theater, and working as a landscaper.[7]

Young Thomas was observed to be a bright and curious child. His mother chronicled his every activity, even organizing these observations and sending what she called, "Tom's Book" to Owen's family in New Zealand. By all accounts Thomas was the center of his mother's world, but that dynamic changed in November 1918 with the birth of his brother, John Paul. Ruth could be cold, and was not reluctant to discipline a headstrong Thomas. In his autobiography, Merton recounts a time that he was sent to bed early, "for stubbornly spelling 'which' without the first 'h': 'w-i-c-h.' I remember brooding about this as an injustice. 'What do they think I am, anyway?' After all, I was still only five years old."[8] As biographer Michael Mott points out, after the birth of his brother, "Love, with both encouragement and correction, had been replaced by cold, intellectual criticism."[9]

Merton's young life was about to face a major crisis when his mother discovered she had stomach cancer. He never knew exactly how long she struggled with her diagnosis while still living at home, but when she was finally admitted to a nearby hospital, the family moved in with Ruth's parents in Douglaston, New York. Thomas would never see his mother again. He was not allowed to see her in the hospital, and sadly Merton always believed

---

5. Mott, *Seven Mountains of Thomas Merton*, 5–6.
6. Mott, *Seven Mountains of Thomas Merton*, 15–16.
7. Mott, *Seven Mountains of Thomas Merton*, 16.
8. Merton, *Seven Storey Mountain*, 10.
9. Mott, *Seven Mountains of Thomas Merton*, 17.

that this was at his mother's request. While Merton knew his mother was sick in the hospital, the six-year-old was not aware how dire the situation actually was until his father handed him a letter from his mother. This note informed the young boy about the grim news. As Merton recalled:

> Then one day Father gave me a note to read. I was very surprised. It was for me personally, and it was in my mother's handwriting. I don't think she had ever written to me before—there had never been any occasion for it. Then I understood what was happening, although, as I remember, the language of the letter was confusing to me. Nevertheless, one thing was quite evident. My mother was informing me, by mail, that she was about to die, and would never see me again.[10]

Sadly, for the rest of his life Merton would think that his mother had decided to deliver this news in a letter, rather than in person. It is now known that Bellevue Hospital had a policy that prevented children from visiting the general wards, and this was Ruth's only way to communicate with her son.[11] Ruth died October 3, 1921. Merton would reflect on this, and other early childhood memories, with the lingering belief that his mother was more cerebral, and less caring and loving, as a parent.[12]

Within a year of Ruth's death Owen decided he needed to make a change and rededicate himself to his painting. He made the decision to move to Bermuda, and took young Thomas with him, leaving his other son John Paul in the care of Ruth's parents in New York. Thomas, now age seven, and his father left for Bermuda in the fall of 1922. While there, Owen met aspiring novelist Evelyn Scott. The two fell in love, despite the fact that Evelyn was married, and they had a tempestuous relationship. Young Thomas did not care for Evelyn at all, and was not bashful in voicing his displeasure to the couple. During this time Owen wrote to a friend stating that "Tom's jealousy and irreconcilableness are perfectly enormous."[13] It appears there was no love lost from Evelyn either. In fact, she confided to a friend that, "Tom is a morbid and possessive kid and Owen is made morbid about Tom

---

10. Merton, *Seven Storey Mountain*, 14.

11. Horan, *Franciscan Heart of Thomas Merton*, 37.

12. In a letter to theologian Rosemary Reuther, whom he had been quarreling with in previous correspondence, Merton wrote, "I promise I won't get up in the air again. I don't know why you frightened me so. ('Cerebral' probably because I resented my mother's intellectuality) (or what I later interpreted as that)" (Merton, *Hidden Ground of Love*, 509).

13. Mott, *Seven Mountains of Thomas Merton*, 33.

through various things that occurred in connection with Ruth. Tom is, and will be until he is big enough to be set adrift, a constant obstacle to piece [sic] of mind."[14] This period was made even more unsettling for Thomas by the fact that Owen would occasionally leave young Thomas with friends so that he could go on trips to sell his art.[15]

After a couple of years in Bermuda, the father and son returned to America so that Owen could exhibit and sell some of his paintings. Flush with money, Owen made plans to return to France to resume his painting with old friends. This time, the eight-year-old Thomas would stay in America with his maternal grandparents, Pop and Bonnemaman. While he was happy to reunite with his grandparents and brother, he missed his father and felt abandoned during this time. Thomas was elated when in July 1925 his father returned to America to fetch him and take him back to France. Many years later Merton reflected on this time in his life, describing that "I realized today after mass what a desperate, despairing childhood I had. Around the age of 7-9-10, when mother was dead and father was in France and Algeria. How much it meant when he came to take me to France. It really saved me."[16] While Thomas was reunited with his father, his younger brother John Paul would once again stay in New York with their grandparents.

In August 1925, Owen and Thomas left for St Antonin, France. Once they arrived and were settled, Thomas attended the Lycée Ingress in Montauban. He lived at the school and took a train on the weekends to spend one day a week with his father.[17] That first summer in France, Thomas faced his first major health crisis, being treated for what was believed to be tuberculosis.[18] Merton was miserable at the Lycée, and in June 1928 his father came to take him out of the school. Merton described his joy and relief to leave, "I looked around me like a man that has had the chains struck from his hands. How the light sang on the brick walls of the prison whose gates had just burst open before me, sprung by some invisible and beneficent power: my escape from the Lycée was, I believe, providential."[19]

14. Mott, *Seven Mountains of Thomas Merton*, 24.
15. Merton, *Seven Storey Mountain*, 19–20.
16. Merton, *Learning to Love*, 6:11–12.
17. Mott, *Seven Mountains of Thomas Merton*, 37.
18. Mott, *Seven Mountains of Thomas Merton*, 37–38
19. Merton, *Seven Storey Mountain*, 60.

Thomas and his father continued to roam, and in 1929 moved to England. There Merton attended a boarding school in Oakham. Owen was still struggling financially, so Thomas's grandfather Pop once again stepped in to help his grandson by paying his tuition.[20] In the summer of 1930, Pop came to visit, and brought news that would have a significant impact on Merton's life. During his stay, Pop took Thomas aside and informed him that he had made arrangements to financially provide for him and his brother for the rest of their lives. Pop[21] had created a trust that contained a diversified portfolio of assets. Thomas and John Paul would own shares of various stocks, as well as property on Long Island and in Coral Gables, Florida. In fact, the Merton brothers would even own an island, Stone Island, off Machiasport, Maine. Thomas would receive an allowance until he turned twenty-one, but Pop would not be administering the trust from New York. Instead, Thomas's godfather, Tom Bennett, would watch over his ward from his London home.[22]

Later, in 1930, tragedy once again visited Merton's life when his father was hospitalized for a brain tumor. In January 1931, one week after Thomas returned to school from Christmas break, his father passed away.[23] At the age of fifteen, Thomas Merton was an orphan. Despite this setback he excelled at school. He corresponded frequently with his grandparents in America, and would spend summers with them. At age seventeen, Thomas faced another health crisis. This time, he became seriously ill after developing blood poisoning from an infected toe, actually coming close to death.[24]

The College Years

After successfully finishing school at Oakham, Merton was accepted into Clare College at Cambridge in 1933. His plan at that time was to complete his education and then enter the diplomatic corps. Unfortunately, his time at Cambridge would prove to be a disaster. Merton quickly took up with

20. Mott, *Seven Mountains of Thomas Merton*, 51.
21. Samuel "Pop" Jenkins worked for a New York publisher, but made his fortune by inventing a kind of picture book that would tell the story of a popular film, using stills from the movie (Mott, *Seven Mountains of Thomas Merton*, 12).
22. Mott, *Seven Mountains of Thomas Merton*, 53.
23. Mott, *Seven Mountains of Thomas Merton*, 55.
24. Mott, *Seven Mountains of Thomas Merton*, 62.

the wrong crowd, ignoring his studies and spending evenings in pubs.[25] At one point during his first semester his raucous behavior may have even included participation in a mock crucifixion.[26] After the first term, his godfather and trust administrator, Tom Bennett, called Thomas to London for a stern lecture. Bennett read Merton the riot act for his poor academic performance and took him to task for racking up debts for tailored clothing, books, alcohol, and trips to nightclubs.[27]

Merton's second semester at Cambridge proved to be no better academically. In addition, his life became even more complicated when, as most biographers believe, he fathered a child. While there is no record that proves this conclusively, the circumstantial evidence is overwhelming that it did in fact occur. That evidence is as follows. At the end of his first year of college, Thomas traveled to New York to visit his grandparents. In June, he received a letter from his godfather Tom Bennett[28] saying that Cambridge was threatening to revoke his scholarship and that it was best if Merton decided to stay in the United States. This was most likely a combination of his abysmal academic performance and the paternity issue. While it is unclear if a paternity suit was actually brought against Merton, it appears that Bennett did in fact arrange some kind of financial settlement with the pregnant woman, using a portion of Merton's trust.[29] In addition, Bennett agreed not to tell Thomas's family about this matter.

This accounting of events is strongly supported by the fact that Merton told many of his friends that he had fathered a child, and as a result had to leave Cambridge. In fact, he told lifelong friend and later Columbia classmate Ed Rice that he had fathered a son, but that both mother and child had been killed during the London Blitz.[30] While Merton may have believed that then, he evidently was not completely sure that had been their fate when he joined the Trappist order in 1944. As a part of making his simple profession, Merton had to write a will that would dispose of any remaining possessions. He still had a portion of his trust, and in the will

---

25. Mott, *Seven Mountains of Thomas Merton*, 75.

26. Mott, *Seven Mountains of Thomas Merton*, 78–79.

27. Mott, *Seven Mountains of Thomas Merton*, 83.

28. Even though Merton would return to England briefly, he remained estranged from Bennett, and the two would never see each other again. Merton considered it to be one of the greatest regrets of his life (Mott, *Seven Mountains of Thomas Merton*, 87–89).

29. Mott, *Seven Mountains of Thomas Merton*, 84–85.

30. Rice, *Man in the Sycamore Tree*, 9.

requested that his sister-in-law receive half of his assets. The other half he bestowed to his godfather Tom Bennett, with the instructions that this portion should be "paid by him to the person mentioned to him in my letters, if that person can be contacted."[31] So, at least in 1944, Merton believed that it was possible that the mother and child may have still been alive.

While the evidence convincingly points to the fact that Merton did indeed father a child, it is a mystery as to who the mother and child were or what happened to them. It is perplexing that despite his prodigious journal keeping and frequent ruminating about his early past, there is not any kind of mention, even an oblique one, about his child. In addition, given Merton's enduring international fame, it is puzzling that no one ever came forward to claim they were the child or mother. In the end, it appears the specifics of this affair will remain a mystery. It seems clear, however, that this episode was a significant factor in encouraging Thomas to stay in America and make a fresh start.

In January 1935, Merton started at Columbia University, and this time he had a successful college experience almost from the beginning.[32] Thomas became involved with campus life and joined the Alpha Delta Phi fraternity. He was also not bashful about regaling his new friends with details of his wild time at Cambridge, bragging that his first sexual experience was with a Viennese prostitute he met at Hyde Park.[33] In addition, he also told many classmates that he had been virtually run out of England for fathering at least one illegitimate child.[34]

Merton also became politically active that year, joining the Young Communist League for a few months. However, by all accounts he was not very actively involved.[35] In addition, Thomas continued to become more involved with school activities, and in 1935 he began writing regularly for *Jester*, Columbia University's humor magazine. In fact, by the end of the next year he became its art editor. Merton served on the yearbook staff and also pursued athletics as a member of the cross country team. Merton seemed to appreciate the second chance he had been given at Columbia and pursued all it had to offer with gusto.[36]

---

31. Mott, *Seven Mountains of Thomas Merton*, 90.
32. Mott, *Seven Mountains of Thomas Merton*, 95.
33. Rice, *Man in the Sycamore Tree*, 36.
34. Mott, *Seven Mountains of Thomas Merton*, 95–96.
35. Mott, *Seven Mountains of Thomas Merton*, 99–101.
36. Mott, *Seven Mountains of Thomas Merton*, 101–2.

Pre-Monastic Period

Merton suffered more loss in his life when his grandfather, Pop, died in October 1936. This was followed, ten months later, by the death of his grandmother, Bonnemaman.[37] Despite these losses he continued to apply himself to his studies and graduated from Columbia University in 1938. Thomas immediately began work on a master's degree and would go on to write his master's thesis on William Blake.[38]

During this time Merton had a chance meeting with a Hindu monk in the summer of 1938 that actually led him to further explore Christianity. At the time this scholar and monk, Mahanambrata Brahmachari, was living in New York with some of Merton's friends. During one of their many conversations Merton asked him what he should read to gain a better understanding of the spiritual and mystical life. Rather than recommending a Hindu text, Brahmachari suggested that Merton read Augustine's *Confessions* and Thomas à Kempis's *The Imitation of Christ*.[39]

In the fall of 1938, after a great deal of study and prayer, Merton decided to convert to Catholicism. While he had been baptized as a child his upbringing was not especially religious. However, Merton had taken a class on Thomas Aquinas at Columbia, and that material, along with the books that Brahmachari had recommended, helped him reach his decision to become Catholic. Shortly after his conversion, in February 1939, he obtained his master's degree and decided to work on his doctorate at Columbia.[40]

The arrival of 1939 marked the start of an interesting period of Merton's life. He was twenty-four and was traveling on what seemed like parallel trajectories. However, as will be seen, these seemingly disparate paths would later become one. On the one hand, Merton was struggling mightily to be a successful writer. He had already written a handful of novels, none of which were accepted for publication. Merton had also been writing poetry for years, and continued to do so during this period. In addition, in 1939 he supplemented his income by writing book reviews for the *New York Herald Tribune* and the *New York Times*.[41] In the Spring of 1940, Merton secured

---

37. Mott, *Seven Mountains of Thomas Merton*, 104.
38. Mott, *Seven Mountains of Thomas Merton*, 112–15.
39. Merton, *Seven Storey Mountain*, 216.
40. Mott, *Seven Mountains of Thomas Merton*, 120–21.
41. Merton, *Seven Storey Mountain*, 257.

Naomi Burton as his literary agent. She would remain his agent, and become a trusted friend and confidant, for the rest of Merton's life.[42]

At this same time, Thomas was trying to determine if he had a religious vocation. Ever since his conversion to Catholicism he had wondered if he was called to the priesthood. Merton had become friendly with his Thomistic philosophy professor, Dan Walsh, and he discussed the possibility of a clerical life with him. Walsh was very encouraging, and in fact told him that he had always believed that Thomas had a religious vocation.[43] Walsh arranged for Merton to meet with local Franciscans, and Thomas submitted an application to enter the Franciscan order in the fall of 1939. Later, in the spring of 1940, Merton traveled to Havana, Cuba—part religious pilgrimage and part indulgence of his wanderlust. While attending mass there he had what he believed was a profound religious experience. Merton described it thusly in his journal, "and so the unshakable certainty, the clear intermediate knowledge that Heaven was right in front of me, struck me like a thunderbolt and went through me like a flash of lightning and seemed to lift me clean up off the earth."[44]

Shortly after returning to America, Merton went to meet again with the Franciscans. This time he felt compelled to tell them the details about his wild past. While there is no clear record as to what he revealed, it is widely believed that it included the fact that he had fathered a child and engaged in a legal settlement.[45] During the conversation Merton was told that it would be best if he withdraw his application to enter the Franciscan order.[46] Crestfallen, Merton decided to keep working on his PhD and secured a job as an English instructor at Saint Bonaventure College in New York. Thomas still felt called to the religious life, even if it would not be as a Franciscan priest, and made plans to become a member of the Third Order of Franciscans, a lay order.[47] In addition, he also bought a breviary, and in his own way attempted to live as a monk in the secular world, following the regimented prayer schedule that one would find in a monastic community.[48]

42. Mott, *Seven Mountains of Thomas Merton*, 148.
43. Mott, *Seven Mountains of Thomas Merton*, 122.
44. Merton, *Secular Journal*, 76–77.
45. Horan, *Franciscan Heart of Thomas Merton*, 70–72.
46. Merton, *Seven Storey Mountain*, 325.
47. Mott, *Seven Mountains of Thomas Merton*, 328.
48. Merton, *Seven Storey Mountain*, 255.

During Christmas break of 1940, Merton met again with his friend and former professor Dan Walsh. Walsh told Merton about a retreat he had recently made at a Trappist[49] monastery in Kentucky, and encouraged Thomas to visit himself.[50] After some deliberation Merton made plans to make a retreat during Holy Week of the upcoming year at Our Lady of Gethsemani Trappist Monastery near Bardstown, Kentucky. He followed through with those plans and made this retreat from April 7–14. He was greatly impressed with the glimpse of daily life there. As he described it in his autobiography:

> I was amazed at the way these monks, who were evidently just plain young Americans from the factories and colleges and farms and high-schools of the various states, were nevertheless absorbed and transformed in the liturgy. The thing that was most impressive was their absolute simplicity. They were concerned with one thing only: doing the things they had to do, singing what they had to sing, bowing and kneeling and so on when it was prescribed, and doing it as well as they could, without fuss or flourish or display. It was all utterly simple and unvarnished and straightforward, and I don't think I had ever seen anything, anywhere, so unaffected, so unself-conscious as these monks.[51]

Merton returned to New York and continued a process of discernment to discover if he truly had a religious vocation through the summer and fall of 1941. It is important to note that during this time Merton was also still actively trying to publish novels. While Thomas was still unclear as to what he should do with his life, in November of that year he became even more uncertain when he was offered a position at Friendship House. Merton had been volunteering at Friendship House, an organization in Harlem dedicated to helping the poor, and was offered a full-time position there.[52] He was clearly at a crossroads as to what to do: work at the Friendship House, continue teaching and his work to become a published writer, or try to live as a monk at Gethsemani. World events soon threatened to make his decision for him.

49. The Trappist Order is also known as the Order of the Cistercians of the Strict Observance. "Since this order was influenced by the Cistercians of a monastery in France called La Trappe, the monks of this order are known as Trappists" (Giroux and Merton, *Letters of Robert Giroux and Thomas Merton*, 24).

50. Merton, *Seven Storey Mountain*, 287–88.

51. Merton, *Seven Storey Mountain*, 361.

52. Merton, *Seven Storey Mountain*, 358–59.

In 1941, the real possibility of being drafted into the military was on the mind of most young men, and Merton was no exception.[53] On December 1, he received a notice from the draft board informing him he had to appear for a second medical examination. Thomas had already undergone one previous exam, but was found to be ineligible for service at that time because of his extensive dental problems. However, as the war in Europe and the Pacific continued to rage, it seemed inevitable that he and his friends would soon be conscripted. With the call for this second medical exam, Merton believed it was likely he would now be deemed fit for service.[54] After more prayer and deliberation, Merton put his affairs in order, obtained a one-month extension for his draft board medical exam, gave away most of his belongings, and left New York. On December 10, 1941, he arrived at Our Lady of Gethsemani.[55]

Early Monastic Life and Loss of His Brother

Merton was accepted into the community as a novice monk, and his lascivious past was not deemed to be a barrier into the monastic life there. The living conditions at the monastery in 1941 were intentionally primitive, with a strict meatless diet. His day consisted of study, prayer, and performing the manual labor that was needed to meet the physical needs of the community, e.g., chopping wood, working in the garden, etc. Merton and his fellow monks had very little privacy. They all slept in a dormitory, with each having a small partitioned area in which to sleep. Merton's bed resembled a wooden bench and his mattress was a straw-filled pallet. Each of the monks took a vow of silence, and it was strictly enforced. Interestingly, the monks had developed their own kind of sign language that included over 400 signs.[56] Shortly before he died he commented on the austere conditions of the monastery upon his initial entry:

> It was inhuman and impossible for a lot of people . . . and there's no point whatever in trying to bring in young people from America now into that kind of thing and make them live the kind of silent life that we lived with: sign language, no heat, bad food, at Lent you had no breakfast and you go out and break rock on the back

---

53. Merton, *Run to the Mountain*, 1:316–17.
54. Merton, *Seven Storey Mountain*, 340–43.
55. Mott, *Seven Mountains of Thomas Merton*, 201.
56. Mott, *Seven Mountains of Thomas Merton*, 209–15.

road like a convict. This is fine, this is a wonderful experience. I'm glad I went through it but I wouldn't want to impose it on anyone else because it's useless.[57]

In July 1942, Merton's brother, John Paul, came to visit the monastery. He had joined the Canadian Air Force and was serving as part of a bomber crew. John Paul asked to receive instruction to become a Catholic, and with the abbot's approval, began a week of intensive instruction about the faith, culminating with his baptism. This week would prove to be a special time for Thomas as it would be the last time he would see his brother. John Paul returned to his unit that was stationed in England, and he was killed on April 16, 1943, when his bomber was shot down over the English Channel. The next day, Merton was called to the abbot's office and given a telegram informing him that his brother was reported missing.[58]

The loss of his brother had a profound impact on Thomas. At the age of twenty-seven, all of his immediate family was dead. In addition, John Paul's death churned up a lifetime of memories and regrets. In his autobiography, Merton reflects upon the guilt and remorse he now felt for mistreating his younger brother when they were children. As Merton describes, these memories of his brother are filled "with poignant compunction at the thought of my own pride and hard-heartedness, and his natural humility and love."[59]

Monk, Writer, and a Search for Peace

When Merton entered the Trappist order, he was unsure about how he could be a writer and monk. He had written a number of poems prior to entering Gethsemani, and these remained in circulation with both his literary agent and friends, who continued searching for a publisher. These efforts paid off when, in November 1944, the poetry collection *Thirty Poems* was published.[60] Soon after this, Merton met with the abbot at that time, Dom Frederick Dunne, and told him he was struggling with whether or not he should write as a monk. His abbot informed him that he should indeed use these talents and continue writing poems and quickly followed up on

---

57. Merton, "Merton Leaves for Asia," 12:01–12:33.
58. Mott, *Seven Mountains of Thomas Merton*, 221–22.
59. Merton, *Seven Storey Mountain*, 24.
60. Mott, *Seven Mountains of Thomas Merton*, 224.

that advice by giving Merton a series of writing assignments, including hagiographies of members of the order, as well as a history of their monastic order. Encouraged by his abbot, and buoyed by having his work published, he began a very prodigious period of writing. In fact, by 1947, Merton noted that he was working on no less than twelve different works.[61] One of these projects became the book that would forever change his life—*The Seven Storey Mountain*. While Merton was still a young man to write an autobiography, his life story and conversion to Catholicism was a compelling one. After being heavily edited by the Trappist censors, it was finally published by Harcourt Brace in October 1948. While the publisher believed it was a good book with an original printing of 5,000 copies, they were not expecting the reception it would receive.[62] In its first three months it sold almost 50,000 copies. Its popularity only increased, at one point selling over 10,000 copies a week. Eventually, 600,000 copies of the original clothback edition were sold.[63] This unlikely bestseller would remain popular, going on to sell millions of copies.

During this time Merton also began to suffer from a host of issues related to his emotional and psychiatric health. This would be a recurring theme for the rest of his life. Merton was ordained a priest on May 26, 1949, and in July of that year Merton passed out while saying Mass. While the heat undoubtedly played a part, biographer Michael Mott believes it was a sign of burnout.[64] He points to the realization Merton expressed in his journals that ordination to the priesthood would not in itself lead to closer union with God, but rather was another stage on the long journey he had been traveling, and would continue to travel on. In addition, Mott argues Merton must have been feeling the pressure of following the success of *The Seven Storey Mountain*.[65] Merton chronicles this tumultuous period himself, writing:

> When the summer of my ordination ended, I found myself face to face with a mystery that was beginning to manifest itself in the depths of my soul and to move me with terror. Do not ask me what it was. I might apologize for it and call it "suffering." The word is not adequate because it suggests physical pain. That is not at

61. Merton, *Sign of Jonas*, 45.
62. Mott, *Seven Mountains of Thomas Merton*, 243.
63. Mott, *Seven Mountains of Thomas Merton*, 247.
64. Mott, *Seven Mountains of Thomas Merton*, 254–55.
65. Mott, *Seven Mountains of Thomas Merton*, 254.

all what I mean. It is true that something had begun to affect my health; but whatever happened to my health was only, it seems to me, an effect of this unthinkable thing that had developed in the depths of my being. And again: I have no way of explaining what it was. It was a sort of slow, submarine earthquake which produced strange commotions on the visible, psychological surface of my life. I was summoned to battle with joy and with fear, knowing in every case that the sense of battle was misleading, that my apparent antagonist was only an illusion, and that the whole commotion was simply the effect of something that had already erupted, without my knowing it, in the hidden volcano.[66]

Merton also began to deal with a number of physical health issues beginning around this time. His gradually deteriorating health would be an issue that he focused more and more upon as he got older. In October and November of 1950 Merton had to go to the hospital in Louisville for surgery on a bone in his nose and treatment for colitis.[67] In addition, during this time it was discovered that Merton had lesions on his lungs that appeared to be scars from his childhood bout with tuberculosis.[68]

Merton also began to actively seek more solitude, and living in community afforded very little of it. Towards this end he began exploring the possibilities of leaving Gethsemeni for another Trappist charter house, or even joining the Carthusian or Camaldoli orders which provided much more solitude for their monks.[69] This desire for change also fits into a broader theme that can be seen in Merton's life. He did not ever feel truly settled, often thinking that if he could only change his surroundings, then he could grow closer to God, would be a better writer, would be his more authentic self, etc. As Merton scholar Robert Daggy put it, Merton "suffered as much as any human from the 'grass is greener' syndrome."[70] Merton himself acknowledged this trait, writing in his journal, "The truth is, something inexplicable draws me away from here, something indefinable makes me uneasy here (I do not say unhappy)—always the old story of 'something missing.' What? Is it something essential? Won't there always be 'something missing'? Yet always that urge to 'go forth,' to leave, to take

66. Merton, *Sign of Jonas*, 230.
67. St. Joseph's Infirmary, on Eastern Parkway, is no longer in existence.
68. Mott, *Seven Mountains of Thomas Merton*, 264.
69. Donald Grayston's *Thomas Merton and the Noonday Demon: The Camaldoli Correspondence*, provides a wonderful account of Merton's efforts to join this Italian order.
70. Merton, *Dancing in the Water of Life*, 5:xv.

off for a strange land and start another life. Perhaps this is inevitable, just a desire one is supposed to have without fulfilling it."[71] Merton's longtime abbot, Dom James Fox, almost always denied Merton's requests to move to a different monastic order or accept invitations to attend conferences. This proved to be a source of no small amount of grief and frustration in Merton's life for decades to come.

The relationship between abbot Dom James Fox and Thomas Merton is a fascinating and complex one, perhaps best characterized by their mutual ambivalence. Dom James was born Harry Vincent Fox on December 10, 1896, in suburban Boston. His family was devoutly Catholic and all of his siblings would go on to have some kind of affiliation with religious communities. Fox was bright and attended Harvard, where he finished his undergraduate degree in three years. He then attended the Harvard Graduate School of Business Administration. Fox was elected abbot in August of 1948 and served in that role for almost twenty years.[72] Many biographers[73] have written at length about the relationship between Merton and his abbot. Perhaps Merton himself most succinctly captured the essence of their relationship in his journal when he wrote, "We are a pair of damned cats."[74] Merton believed that the abbot went out of his way to prevent him from exploring the opportunity for more solitude outside of Gethsemani and attending conferences. He often saw these actions as the petty exercise of authority. Dom James, on the other hand, believed he was acting responsibly in exercising his authority, and was in large part saving Merton from himself, as well as taking care of the rest of the community. To show both men's point of view, I have selected representative writing samples from each.

Merton wrote extensively in his journals about his frustration with his abbot, but also made them known to Dom James himself. I quote at length from a letter he wrote to him in 1959 that demonstrates the degree of frustration and resentment he often felt towards his abbot:

> I fully recognize your right to refuse permission for a leave of absence. In this you were following your conscience and within your

---

71. Merton, *Search for Solitude*, 285.

72. Lipsey, *Make Peace*, 9–15.

73. Roger Lipsey's *Make Peace before the Sun Goes Down: The Long Encounter of Thomas Merton and His Abbot, James Fox* focuses exclusively on this relationship and provides a fascinating, comprehensive, and balanced accounting of their relationship.

74. Merton, *Learning to Love*, 6:108.

rights. But I wonder about the way in which you have done everything possible to prevent me obtaining permission from anyone and in any way whatsoever. I do not deny you this right, but in point of fact it seems to me to represent an arbitrary and tyrannical spirit. Are you not so intent on your own views, in this matter, that you are willing to stifle the Holy Ghost in a soul? Do you not have an inordinate tendency to interfere in the workings of conscience and to suppress by violence those desires and ideals which run counter to your policies? Do you not tend to assume that your own policies represent the last word in the spiritual perfection of every one of your subjects? . . . I have always striven to be perfectly obedient to legitimate commands in the external forum, but I beg the right to form my conscience according to the guidance of my directors, in the internal forum, without demands that I follow your directions and no other. I hope you understand this rightly as a humble and filial petition.[75]

Dom James saw things differently. In the following portion of a letter to the superior of the entire order, Dom Gabriel Sortais, Fox shows he believed he was acting to help Merton:

> Father Louis (the name Merton took when he joined the order) knows that his troubles do not come from his Trappist surroundings in general, and Gethsemani in particular. He knows, because he practically admitted it to me, that his problems are all inside himself. But as neurotics usually do, they blame everybody and everything else for their interior suffering. His problem is that he would like to be without any restraint or discipline over him, so that he could always do what he wished. But if he were in such a position, where would his spiritual life be? Where would his sanctification be? And he knows that very well.[76]

Fox also had the well-being of his community and fellow monks to consider, and he saw Merton's departure to another monastic community as being problematic. Merton was well thought of and admired by many, especially younger, monks. In describing the impact on them, Fox wrote, "They look upon him as an oracle of spirituality and lean heavily upon him for their guidance in the spiritual life. If he ever were to leave here, it would be a source of great scandal to our young professed and would betray them into the spirit of instability and change. I can hardly picture what the results

---

75. Merton, *Witness to Freedom,* 216.
76. Lipsey, *Make Peace,* 65.

of his change from here would be."⁷⁷ It is important to point out that while the relationship was often contentious, there was also a bond of mutual respect and care. It is no small irony to a visitor at the Gethsemani cemetery today to see Dom James buried next to Merton's grave.

In 1953, in an effort to accommodate Merton's desire for more solitude, Dom James allowed him to use an abandoned toolshed on the monastery grounds, dubbed St. Anne's. He was only allowed to spend a few hours a day there, and it was not his to use exclusively.⁷⁸ Merton continued to long for greater solitude and to live more of an eremitical lifestyle. In 1955, Dom James offered to let him live in a nearby fire tower. This would provide Merton the solitude he had been asking for, while also providing a valuable service to the monastic community and surrounding county. The only stipulation was that Merton could do no writing of any kind, could not keep a notebook, have a typewriter, etc. for the next five years. When faced with this reality Merton quickly dropped those plans, and in fact volunteered for a newly vacant position of Master of Novices, teaching the new monks.⁷⁹

Merton enjoyed his work with the novices and by all accounts did a fine job with their instruction.⁸⁰ His instruction focused on their practical spiritual formation rather than solely academic matters.⁸¹ During this time Merton also continued writing, his active prayer schedule, and other assigned tasks at the monastery. In addition, he was able to receive books from friends, and was a voracious reader, devouring several books at one time. His interests ranged from world literature to Western and Eastern theology and even to nuclear physics.⁸²

On March 15, 1958, Merton had what he considered to be a profound religious experience. While in Louisville meeting with a printer about a monastic publication, he came to a crowded downtown intersection, Fourth and Walnut. Merton, who had spent most of the last seventeen years separated from the rest of world, suddenly felt connected, in a real and intimate way, to the rest of humanity. As he described sometime later:

---

77. Grayston, *Thomas Merton and the Noonday Demon*, 123–24.
78. Mott, *Seven Mountains of Thomas Merton*, 274.
79. Cooper, *Thomas Merton's Art of Denial*, 56–57.
80. Mott, *Seven Mountains of Thomas Merton*, 288–89.
81. Grayston, *Thomas Merton and the Noonday Demon*, 27.
82. Mott, *Seven Mountains of Thomas Merton*, 307.

> In Louisville, at the corner of Fourth and Walnut, in the center of the shopping district, I was suddenly overwhelmed with the realization that I loved all those people, that they were mine and I theirs, that we could not be alien to one another even though we were total strangers. It was like waking from a dream of separateness, of spurious self-isolation in a special world, the world of renunciation and supposed holiness. The whole illusion of a separate holy existence is a dream. Not that I question the reality of my vocation, or of my monastic life: but the conception of "separation from the world" that we have in the monastery too easily presents itself as a complete illusion: the illusion that by making vows we become a different species of being, pseudoangels, "spiritual men," men of interior life, what have you.[83]

This experience had a profound and long-lasting effect on Merton's life. While he would continue to write about contemplation and solitude, this reawakening to the broader world caused him to focus on a variety of social ills that humanity was facing. In addition, during this time Merton also continued his exploration of Zen and Buddhism.

The year 1960 saw the birth of new friendships in Merton's life. He began seeing a Louisville psychiatrist, Jim Wygal, for a regular series of psychoanalysis. This relationship would change from that of doctor and patient to one of friends. These regular visits meant Merton would be making more regular trips to Louisville, which increasingly included excursions to Wygal's house to listen to jazz records as well as to jazz clubs.[84]

Merton also continued to struggle with his emotional health. In his journals, he candidly chronicles these problems:

> And so my own neurosis runs like a sore, and I know it, and see it, and see that I am helpless to do anything about it! And am, of course, guilty. So it is that the Christian and monastic mind is admirably fitted to be a seed ground of neurosis. This is at once a weakness and a strength. Unfortunately I can't imagine, for the moment, where to find any kind of strength in this futility.[85]

Continuing to struggle with the same issues, less than a week later he wrote, "Anyway, I am worn down. I am easily discouraged. The depressions are deeper, more frequent. I am near fifty. People think I am happy."[86]

83. Merton, *Conjectures of a Guilty Bystander*, 156–57.
84. Moses, *Divine Discontent*, 4.
85. Merton, *Turning Toward the World*, 4:321.
86. Merton, *Turning Toward the World*, 4:323.

Why Merton?

The Hermitage Years and the Affair

There was a movement at Gethsemani to host representatives from other Christian faiths in an effort to foster a growing spirt of ecumenism. In order to meet those needs, while avoiding unnecessary disruption of the routine of the community, plans were made to construct a small building that was to serve as a conference center on the monastery grounds. Before construction began Merton's abbot agreed that this space would also be an ideal place for Merton to achieve the solitude he craved. Initially, Dom James would only allow him to visit it periodically. However, over time Merton was gradually allowed to spend more time at the concrete block building that would, in time, become his permanent home: Our Lady of Mount Carmel Hermitage.

During these years Merton also continued to battle a variety of medical issues. These continuing health problems, and the reality that he was no longer a healthy young man, are clearly expressed in a journal entry around this time. Merton had found an old photograph of himself playing rugby at Cambridge, and he writes:

> I can see that that was a different body from the one I have now—one entirely young and healthy, one that did not know sickness, weakness, anguish, tension, fatigue—a body totally assured of itself and without care . . . And now what kind of a body! An arthritic hip; a case of chronic dermatitis on my hands for a year and a half (so that I have to wear gloves); sinusitis, chronic ever since I came to Kentucky; lungs always showing up some funny shadow or other on ex-rays (though not lately); perpetual diarrhea and a bleeding anus; most of my teeth gone; most of my hair gone; a chewed-up vertebra in my neck which causes my hands to go numb and my shoulder to ache—and for which I sometimes need traction . . . [87]

Merton struggled with neck and back problems for several years and conservative care could no longer provide relief. Merton was admitted to St. Joseph's Infirmary in March 1966 for back surgery. While recovering there he met a student nurse, "M," from Cincinnati.[88] The two struck up a

---

87. Merton, *Dancing in the Water of Life* 5:326.

88. Merton's account of this relationship in his journals is one sided, and its editors have rightly decided to keep this woman's identity private, referring to her simply as "M." While her name has been published in some biographies, I also choose the same moniker, "M."

friendship during his stay there, and that relationship would continue after he returned to Gethsemani. In fact, it quickly became a romantic one, with elaborately arranged meetings in Louisville. The two also supplemented their time together with phone calls and voluminous letter writing, with each declaring their love for the other. While this affair only lasted several months, it had a profound impact on the last years of his life. Merton believed that he had finally found feminine love, something that he thought he had never experienced in his life.[89]

Merton's relationship with M helped reaffirm that his role in this world was that of a monk. No matter how dysfunctional at times he found his monastic order to be, his place was in it, not out in the secular world. While there is no evidence that Merton ever seriously considered leaving the religious life, this was certainly the time to do it if he was ever so inclined. This internationally famous author had found the love of a beautiful and intelligent woman, who was prepared to run away with him and get married; if he would only ask.[90] Instead, Merton chose the familiarity of his cloister and his calling to live as a priest and monk. While Thomas and M continued to exchange sporadic letters and phone calls into 1968, it was, for all practical purposes, over in the fall of 1966.[91]

Merton resumed his usual activities of writing and visits with guests to his hermitage. In addition, keeping up with letter writing was increasingly difficult. He was a prolific letter writer, exchanging over 10,000 letters with approximately 2,100 people.[92] This included religious figures (e.g., Karl Rahner, Rosemary Ruether, Thich Nhat Hanh, D. T. Suzuki), those devoted to social justice and peace (e.g., Dorothy Day, Daniel Berrigan), other writers (e.g., Boris Pasternak, John Howard Griffin), and celebrities (e.g., Joan Baez and members of the Kennedy family). During this time Merton was increasingly focused on issues outside the monastery. He continued writing about the war in Vietnam, nuclear proliferation, and a host of problems and social ills facing society in the mid-1960s.

On September 7, 1967, Merton received news that would considerably change his life. The long-serving abbot, Dom James Fox, was resigning from

---

89. Merton, *Dancing in the Water of Life*, 5:259–60.
90. Merton, *Learning to Love*, 6:54–55.
91. Mott, *Seven Mountains of Thomas Merton*, 468.

92. Gardner, *Only Mind Worth Having*, 2–3. Hundreds of these have been published in a variety of books, with many others collected at the Thomas Merton Center at Bellarmine University.

that position and Merton was overjoyed about the change in leadership. Interestingly, he was concerned enough at the prospect of being chosen to lead the community that he posted a tongue-in-cheek letter, "MY CAMPAIGN PLATFORM," writing that he was not fit for the job because he was not a good administrator, had no business acumen, and was not "equipped to spend the rest of my life arguing about complete trivialities with one hundred and twenty-five slightly confused and anxiety ridden monks."[93] His observations about his fellow monks offended several members of his community.

An abbotical election was held in January of 1968, and Fr. Flavian Burns was elected the new head of the monastic community. Merton was elated, as he had taught Burns when he was a novice monk. Merton's horizons soon opened wide when the new abbot granted him permission to travel to the types of conferences he had been denied in the past.

Merton accepted an invitation from the Aide á l'Implantation Monastique organization, a Benedictine group that worked for monastic renewal. They planned a conference in Bangkok in December 1968, and Merton was invited to be a speaker. While in Asia, Merton would have an opportunity to immerse himself in Buddhism and explore other monastic traditions, all with the hope that he would return home and share those learnings with his own community. In addition, Merton was also granted permission to visit various monastic communities in the United States.[94] In May, he spent two weeks at monasteries on the California coast and New Mexican desert before his trip abroad.

That old and persistent feeling of restlessness also returned. Around this time Merton was finding that life at his hermitage was not as fulfilling as it once was. The solitude he had longed for was increasingly disturbed by a parade of visitors—many invited, some others not. Word had spread that Merton was living apart from the community, and many people discovered ways to avoid the monastery gates to reach his hermitage. These interlopers included spiritual seekers, students and clergy interested in Merton's work, and occasionally the mentally deranged. He humorously described one of these encounters in his journal, "The other night when it was too hot to go to bed, I was sitting up with nothing on but a pair of underpants when a

---

93. Mott, *Seven Mountains of Thomas Merton*, 503–4.
94. Horan, *Franciscan Heart of Thomas Merton*, 50.

couple of admirers suddenly appeared in front of the cottage. I told them to get the hell out, thereby once again ruining my image."[95]

The End of the Journey

In July of 1968, more of his time was occupied with preparation for his trip to Asia. There were many details to sort out, including trips to Louisville for required inoculations.[96] On September 10, he left Gethsemani to begin his journey. His itinerary was somewhat open-ended, with his abbot agreeing to consider changes to his schedule based on other offers to travel that might be made while on the trip.[97] What no one could have known was that this was the last day Thomas Merton would spend at Gethsemani.

Merton first spent time at monastic communities in New Mexico, Alaska, and California. He gave conferences to the other monks and religious and also explored surrounding areas for possible future hermitages.[98] Finally, on October 15, he set off for Asia. In his journal Merton describes his elation at finally embarking on a trip that he had dreamed of for years:

> The moment of take-off was ecstatic. The dewy wing was suddenly covered with rivers of cold sweat running backward. The window wept jagged shining courses of tears. Joy. We left the ground—I with Christian mantras and a great sense of destiny, of being at last on my true way after years of waiting and wondering and fooling around . . . I am going home, to the home where I have never been in this body . . .[99]

Merton arrived in Bangkok, and after a couple days of rest, he left for Calcutta. Once there he was overwhelmed with the crush of people and grinding poverty.[100] A trip to New Dehli and other parts of India soon followed. On November 1, he took a train from New Delhi to Dharamsala, where the Dalai Lama resided. Months before, arrangements had been made for the two to meet. Over the course of a week they met on three separate occasions. Merton recorded in his journals that the Dalai Lama

---

95. Merton, *Other Side of the Mountain*, 7:129.
96. Merton, *Other Side of the Mountain*, 7:143–46.
97. Mott, *Seven Mountains of Thomas Merton*, 537.
98. Mott, *Seven Mountains of Thomas Merton*, 541.
99. Merton, *Other Side of the Mountain*, 7:205.
100. Merton, *Other Side of the Mountain*, 7:216.

told him he was familiar with his writings. After discussing Merton's interest in Tibetan mysticism, the Dalai Lama recommended that he meet with a qualified Tibetan scholar who could unite study and practice.[101]

Two days later, Merton and the Dalai Lama met again. Merton notes that most of their discussions during this visit centered around Eastern and Western comprehension of knowledge and understanding. However, their meeting included more than a discussion about epistemology. Interestingly, this encounter also included a demonstration of the Tibetan meditation posture by the Dalai Lama. Merton describes that this second meeting went very well and that both men had enjoyed themselves, with a promise to meet again in two days.[102] On November 5, the two met again for the last time. They continued their conversation about the various approaches to knowledge, as well as comparing details of the daily lives of Western and Buddhist monks. Merton believed this was the best of their three visits and wrote in his journal that "it was a very warm and cordial discussion and at the end I felt we had become very good friends and were somehow quite close to one another. I feel great respect and fondness for him as a person and I believe, too, that there is a real spiritual bond between us."[103]

On November 29, Merton arrived in Colombo, Ceylon (now Sri Lanka). A few days later he would have a religious experience that is reminiscent of the one that he had at Fourth and Walnut in Louisville, as well as the one in Cuba some twenty-eight years before. It is similar in terms of how it seemed to open his eyes to a new understanding about the nature of being and his place in the world. This occurred on December 4, when Merton had an opportunity to visit Polonnaruwa to see the famous statues of the Buddhas. Merton described this experience a few days later in his traveling journal. While it is a lengthy entry, it is important to let Merton speak for himself in his description of this event:

> Looking at these figures I was suddenly, almost forcibly, jerked clean out of the habitual, half-tied vision of things, and an inner clearness, clarity, as if exploding from the rocks themselves, became evident and obvious. The queer evidence of the reclining figure, the smile, the sad smile of Ananda standing with arms folded (much more "imperative" than Da Vinci's Mona Lisa because completely simple and straightforward). The thing about all this

---

101. Merton, *Asian Journal*, 112–13.
102. Merton, *Asian Journal*, 113.
103. Merton, *Asian Journal*, 125.

is that there is no puzzle, no problem, and really no "mystery." All problems are resolved and everything is clear, simply because what matters is clear. The rock, all matter, all life, is charged with dharmakaya—everything is emptiness and everything is compassion. I don't know when in my life I have ever had such a sense of beauty and spiritual validity running together in one aesthetic illumination. Surely, with Mahabalipuram and Polonnaruwa my Asian pilgrimage has come clear and purified itself. I mean, I know and have seen what I was obscurely looking for. I don't know what else remains but I have now seen and have pierced through the surface and have got beyond the shadow and the disguise. This is Asia in its purity, not covered over with garbage, Asian or European or American, and it is clear, pure, complete. It says everything; it needs nothing. And because it needs nothing it can afford to be silent, unnoticed, undiscovered.[104]

It would have been interesting to see how Merton would have processed and reflected further on this experience as he continued his trip and eventually returned to Gethsemani. Unfortunately, that was not meant to be as he would be dead within the week.

Merton finally returned to Bangkok after a brief stop in Singapore, on December 7. The conference started two days later, and on December 10, 1968, Merton gave a presentation entitled "Marxism and Monastic Perspectives."[105] He ended his remarks by saying, "so I will disappear from view and we can all have a Coke or something. Thank you very much."[106] Those were his last words recorded or written. After lunch Merton returned to the cottage that he and a few other priests were sharing at the conference center. Later that day other priests found Merton lying on the floor with a fan partially covering his body. A doctor soon arrived and pronounced him dead at the age of fifty-three. An investigation was hastily done and determined that he had suffered sudden heart failure. Merton had entered Gethsemani on that date, exactly twenty-seven years earlier.

Thomas Merton is a remarkably complex figure. As a cloistered monk, it could appear that he lived a life foreign to most of us, existing on the margins of society. However, through his writings we discover a man that is just like us in the important ways. His was a life of joy and grief, contentment and longing, love and loss—it was a full life.

104. Merton, *Asian Journal*, 233–36.
105. Mott, *Seven Mountains of Thomas Merton*, 563.
106. Mott, *Seven Mountains of Thomas Merton*, 564.

Why Merton?
Merton and the State of the World and Church

So many of Merton's critiques of our society and religion are as relevant today as they were when they were written. While some of the particulars have changed, his broader points still ring true. In the remaining part of this chapter I explore Merton's writings that address challenges the world and church faced and the role the individual Christian witness would play.

Merton offered a clear and sober assessment of the secular society of his time. He worried that it was fast approaching a point where it might "plunge to its own ruin" unless it made large-scale changes.[107] Merton believed that the values promoted by popular culture ultimately lead to frustration and alienation from other people and from God. He described a prevalent kind of "moral confusion" that created a host of societal problems including "alcoholism, pornography, drug addiction . . . which are only symptomatic, but not the real trouble."[108]

Merton, writing decades before the emergence of social media, warns that in our society it can be difficult to ever authentically know others. Popular culture defines what it means to be happy and successful. In order to conform to those ideals we often create personas that match those definitions. Thus we encounter an idealized version of someone, rather than the actual person. Merton writes that one often finds that he or she is "related not to flesh and blood human beings with the same freedom, responsibility, and conflicts as himself, but with the idealized typological images: . . . the president, the sports star, the teen singer."[109]

Merton also recognizes that immersion in our hyper-consumptive society can lead to frustration and, in many cases, estrangement from our true selves. Within this system there is a tendency to define an individual's value by how and what one consumes. Merton argues that the role of consumer often replaces one's individuality and "is then reduced to a state of permanent nonentity and tutelage in which his more or less abstract presence in society is tolerated only if he conforms, remains a smoothly functioning automaton, an uncomplaining and anonymous element in the great reality of the market."[110] He writes that this consumer culture

---

107. Merton, *Seeds of Destruction*, 10.
108. Merton, *Contemplation in a World of Action*, 31.
109. Merton, *Seeds of Destruction*, 186.
110. Merton, *Contemplation in a World of Action*, 31.

> tries to keep us dazzled with euphoria in a bright cloud of lively and joy-loving slogans. Yet nothing is more empty and more dead, nothing is more insultingly insincere and destructive than the vapid grins on the billboards and the moron beatitude in the magazines which assure us that we are all in bliss right now . . . I think the constant realization that we are exhausting our vital spiritual energy in a waste of shame, the inescapable disgust at the idolatrous vulgarity of our commercial milieu . . . is one of the main sources of our universal desperation.[111]

This sentiment has never been truer as social media "influencers" rave about their latest purchase of jeans, pots and pans, or bed linens, and describe how this "stuff" profoundly changed their lives for the better.

This alienation, from ourselves and others, inevitably leads to what Merton describes as frustration and despair because it prevents people from pursuing those things that provide real fulfillment. While some people recognize the vacuousness of that path, most fall into a "mindless and routine conformity to the demands of a highly organized social machine."[112] Merton notes that the burgeoning countercultural movement of his time was a sign that people were waking up to, and rejecting, this kind of superficial, consumer-oriented life. He points to the popularity of LSD, which was tried by as many as two million Americans by the end of his life, as a sign that people were seeking something deeper than the shallow existence found in popular culture.[113] In making this point he writes that "whatever one may think of psychedelic drugs, as a sociological fact they clearly indicate that the desire for inner experience is not something buried in the medieval past."[114]

Merton and the State of Religion

Merton wrote and spoke about the state of religion during the last decade of his life, and many of those insights are relevant today. He points out that many Christians refuse to accept the fact that we are living in a post-Christian world and act as if the church still has the same kind of power and influence that it had in the past. Merton also notes that many Christians believe that the secular world despises and persecutes them. However,

---

111. Merton, *Faith and Violence*, 68.
112. Merton, *Contemplation in a World of Action*, 58.
113. Pollan, *How to Change Your Mind*, 200.
114. Merton, *Contemplation in a World of Action*, 107.

he argues that Christianity has become so irrelevant that the wider secular society can't even muster up the interest or energy to hate it. Merton was not disheartened by the church's diminished stature. Instead, he saw it as an opportunity for Christians, writing that "it is really a liberation. We no longer have to take ourselves so abominably seriously as 'Christians' with a public and capital 'C.' We can give a little more thought to the reality of our vocation and bother less with the image which we show to the world."[115]

In assessing the state of Christianity of that time Merton also responded to a theological movement that was growing in popularity—the Death of God. While it no longer garners the attention it once did it is important to examine Merton's response to it because it includes his critique of society and Christianity at that time and illustrates how Merton continually engaged with thought which was different than his own. There were several Death of God theologians, but Merton focused on the writings of French theologian Gabriel Vahanian. The Death of God concept was not the atheism of the nineteenth century; instead it was a post-Christian iconoclasm that abandoned the search for a transcendent God. Vahanian defines iconoclasm here as "an attempt, not to re-create, but to transfigure the world and man's situation in it, including all the everyday aspects of existence."[116]

Merton believed the growth of this movement was a sign that people were yearning for something not readily accessible in religion at that time.[117] Vahanian and other like-minded theologians proclaimed that humanity is completely incapable of grasping or even wanting some kind of divine revelation. The Death of God was a recognition that in society God was no longer considered necessary and his existence was not taken for granted.[118] These theologians believed that the God the church had presented to the world was, as Merton describes, "completely unreal—a mere convenience, serving man's purposes, a social commodity, a cosmic tranquilizer to be packaged and marketed along with any other product . . . like next year's Chevrolet."[119] The Death of God theologians also argued that the Christian church had conflated its ideals with those of Western culture.[120]

115. Merton, *Faith and Violence*, 116–17.
116. Vahanian, *Wait Without Idols*, xi.
117. Merton, *Faith and Violence*, 163.
118. Vahanian, *Wait Without Idols*, 46.
119. Merton, *Faith and Violence*, 191.
120. Vahanian, *Wait Without Idols*, 24.

As Merton describes it, "the whole problem of the salvation of the world could be reduced to the task of turning everybody else into a more or less plausible replica of Western man . . . to save the soul of the African one needed only to baptize him and enslave him, thus killing two birds with one stone: gaining black souls for Heaven and making a fortune out of the Alabama cotton."[121]

These Death of God proponents argued that the only possible authentic religious experience is one of experiencing God's absence.[122] The symbols and myths of traditional theology not only fail to resonate with a modern believer, they have instead made it "all the more difficult for him to find any meaning whatever in the concept of God."[123] Finally, the Death of God theologians believed it was important to ensure "the reality of the living God is free from the cultural concepts and other institutions that attempt to objectify and domesticate it."[124] They predicted that new concepts of God would be developed as humans continue to search for the answers to life's ultimate questions "and a new era begins when a new religiosity appears, rising from the empty tomb of the dead God."[125]

While Merton did agree with some of this movement's critiques of secular culture and religion, he rejected its overall approach and conclusions. He succinctly summarized his attitude, writing that this kind of theology was "often mere sophomoric anti-religion and anti-clericalism, and seems to end by subjecting man more completely and more arbitrarily to the massive domination of post-Christian secularism."[126] Merton did recognize, however, that attitudes towards faith and organized religion were changing in his lifetime and that Christians and the church of the future would have to adapt.

Merton also made a broader critique of religion. He acknowledged that "it is no secret that the Church finds herself in crisis."[127] Part of that problem was the increasing tendency to treat religion like a commodity. He believed that the commoditization of religion turned faith into a mass-marketed bundle of clichés to be sold like any other product. Merton writes that when this occurs people are:

121. Merton, *Faith and Violence*, 191.
122. Merton, *Faith and Violence*, 191–92.
123. Merton, *Faith and Violence*, 191–92.
124. Vahanian, *Wait Without Idols*, 231.
125. Vahanian, *Wait Without Idols*, 231.
126. Merton, *Faith and Violence*, 197–98.
127. Merton, *Seeds of Destruction*, 10.

urged in the most shallow, importunate, tasteless and meaningless ways, that they had to go to church or synagogue or conventicle of some sect. Just get into the nearest conventicle as fast as your legs can carry you, brother, and get on your knees and worship; we don't give a hoot how you do it or why you do it, but you've got to get in there and worship, brother, because the advertising industry says so and it is written right on the napkin in the place where you eat your fallout lettuce sandwich.[128]

Merton goes even further in stating that popular religion of that time had, to a great extent, "betrayed man's inner spirit and turned him over . . . to turn the mill of a self-frustrating and self-destroying culture."[129] Merton doesn't question the sincerity of theologians or preachers but does find fault with the underlying "worn-out presuppositions with which they are content to operate."[130] He argues that religion at that time was too focused on "wrong or irrelevant issues" while ignoring the more pressing ones. Merton writes: "apart from a few token issues that are defended with complete intransigence, like birth control, sexual morality, etc., the whole trend seems to be toward the supine acceptance of the most secular, the most debased, the most empty of worldly standards. In this case the acceptance of nuclear war."[131]

Merton admits that Christians owe the secular world an apology. While Christians are called to love and respect their neighbor they have been too quick to reject secular society, waiting for it to become something worth saving. He writes that too many Christians focus on people who don't live and believe the way that they think "a good Christian" should. Merton points out that this fixation actually reveals an inadequacy of their own faith. God can and does redeem the world, even without the help of what he calls "self-righteous Christians." Finally, Merton writes that some Christians become obsessed with imposing their will on others. When this occurs these Christians are simply using "the Gospel as a gimmick for self-justification."[132]

Merton also writes about the kind of faith that many self-professed Christians actually espouse. Martin Marty's 1964 book, *Varieties of Unbelief*, sparked his interest in the subject. Marty argues that while many

---

128. Merton, *Seeds of Destruction*, 186.
129. Merton, *Faith and Violence*, 116.
130. Merton, *Faith and Violence*, 116.
131. Merton and Cardenal, *From the Monastery to the World*, 125.
132. Merton, *Faith and Violence*, 207.

claim to have faith in God they instead have faith in a force that guarantees security and their way of life. They are not interested in a God who calls for some kind of sacrifice or demands that they transcend their own self-interest. Instead, they seek a god who delivers and safeguards prosperity and promotes the values of individualism, nationalism, and progress. Merton sums up Marty's findings, writing that "what passes for Christian faith among many Americans is perhaps less respectable, intellectually and spiritually, than the concerned atheism of those whose unbelief implies the courageous assumption of loneliness, dread and risk."[133] Here one can see a precursor for the kind of Moralistic Therapeutic Deism that was identified in young people at the turn of this century.

The Church in Diaspora

Despite Merton's critique of Christianity he did not think that it would become extinct. He did, however, believe that the cultural influence of the church would continue to decrease. Merton writes that for many Christians the "normal" state of the world was the medieval one in which the church was all powerful, in both private and public life. These Christians believe it is their task to turn back the clock and restore that kind of order to the world. Merton rejected this impulse to reclaim the past and agreed with German theologian Karl Rahner who asserted that the institutional church would most likely find itself existing in a diaspora.[134]

Merton did not believe that acknowledging the church's waning influences was a sign of defeat. Instead, he saw it as the clear-eyed rejection of the belief that "with a little more zeal, a little more energy, a few more mass movements and smarter use of mass-media, the Church will very likely take over everything and definitively convert the City of Man into the City

---

133. Merton, *Faith and Violence*, 201.

134. Merton presents Rahner's argument in his book *Seeds of Destruction* and in journal articles without much editorial comment, being somewhat vague as to how much he agreed with Rahner. However, Merton's correspondence shows that he most certainly did agree with him. First, Merton is explicit about it in a letter to Dan Berrigan, writing that he has "been reading and reviewing Rahner's latest book and agree with him about what he calls the diaspora situation" (Merton, *Hidden Ground of Love*, 80–81). In addition, in a 1964 letter to Rahner, Merton wrote "needless to say, I am in hearty agreement with your book and share with you the deep concern for a new and less rigidly institutional view of the Church, the concern that has been raised by the situation of the Church in her true 'diaspora,' the countries where unpleasant realities must be faced (and are not always faced)" (Merton, *Hidden Ground of Love*, 497).

of God—on a medieval pattern."[135] Merton believed that the institutional church would persist, with a diminishing cultural influence, serving as a sign of contradiction to the secular world.

Thomas Merton and the Individual Witness

Importantly, Merton also writes that since the church will play a lesser role in society the individual Christian will be called to "take original and creative action in his own sphere."[136] The duty of spreading the good news will remain an essential component of being Christian. Merton argues that if the non-Christian is invited to "enter with us into a ghetto of antiquated customs and rituals, dominated by a censorious theology which seems grimly opposed to everything he experiences as 'life' he will turn away from us in despair."[137] Now, in this increasingly secularized world, Christians must find new ways to share the gospel message.

Merton builds on this idea by affirming the vital role the laity will play in the coming years. He writes:

> With all these obstacles the Church, even though to some extent reduced to silence, will continue her missionary activity, but now in radically new forms in which the purity of the individual witness will take precedence over everything else. Not only will the Church continue to preach the Gospel, without defeatism and without rancor, she will remain on the offensive. But this "offensive" will be completely independent of human power, relying, like that of the apostles, on the power of God.[138]

The last two chapters highlighted a number of recent religious changes in the United States, along with a growing disregard of facts and truth in favor of opinions. It is within this context, especially with the declining membership and influence of the church, that the role of the individual witness has never been more important and necessary. Therefore, in the chapters that follow I identify ways that Merton's life and writings can serve as a model for Christians to live in the world today and be that witness.

---

135. Merton, *Seeds of Destruction*, 187.
136. Merton, "Monk in the Diaspora," 292.
137. Merton, "Monk in the Diaspora," 296.
138. Merton, *Seeds of Destruction*, 198.

4

Merton and the Individual Witness, Part I

WE ARE NOW READY to bring Merton into contact with our current world with the hope that his life and writings can provide a model for individual Christian witnessing in society today.

ENGAGE WITH THE WORLD

Merton can help us answer a fundamental question: How should Christians engage with our post-Christian and post-truth society? There have been a number of popular books recently written that offer various suggestions. For example, should we follow Rod Dreher's call in *The Benedict Option* to make a tactical retreat from the world, focusing on the creation of Christian communities, or lean towards Julian Carrón's advice in *Disarming Beauty* to embrace it and be the Christ event in the world today? *The Benedict Option* was described by one *New York Times* columnist as being "the most discussed and most important religious book of the decade."[1] Dreher, a columnist and Eastern Orthodox Christian, believes that Christianity has been in a steady decline for decades. He cites many of the same statistics and trends about institutional church membership discussed in the first chapter of this book, including research about the pervasiveness of Moralistic Therapeutic Deism. Dreher believes that not only has Christianity lost its influence on society, it also faces increased hostility. It is within this

---

1. Brooks, "Benedict Option," para. 4.

context that he grimly proclaims that "the light of Christianity is flickering out all over the West. There are people alive today who may live to see the effective death of Christianity within our civilization."[2] Dreher declares that Christians have lost the so-called culture war, with the Supreme Court's decision affirming the right to same-sex marriage as the watershed event in that battle.

Dreher disagrees with some conservatives who believe it is possible to turn the tide on those societal trends that he identifies as being antithetical to Christianity. Instead, he calls for a deliberate retreat from society and the creation of communities to foster Christian values. As he writes, "rather than wasting energy and resources fighting unwinnable political battles, we should instead work on building communities, institutions, and networks of resistance that can outwit, outlast, and eventually overcome the occupation."[3] Dreher describes this approach as the Benedict Option, "a strategy that draws on the authority of Scripture and the wisdom of the ancient church to embrace 'exile in place' and form a vibrant counterculture."[4] Benedict Option Christians look to Scripture and the monastic Rule of St. Benedict for ways to cultivate Christian practices and communities. Towards this end Christian parents are encouraged to take their children out of public schools, homeschooling them or creating new Christian schools with curriculums based on classic Western literature. In addition, Dreher recommends that Christians do business with other like-minded Christians as much as possible, even if it costs more. To support these efforts Christians are encouraged to create their own employment networks.

On the other end of the spectrum, Julian Carrón, priest and leader of Communion and Liberation—a Catholic group dedicated to education and missionary work—calls for full Christian engagement with the world. He agrees with Dreher and many others who believe that people no longer have a shared worldview, which led to "a collapse of the certainties that for centuries were the basis of our coexistence."[5] This results in a kind of "lethargy and existential boredom" that is pervasive today.[6]

Carrón believes that past Christian attempts to affect change in the world have been unsuccessful. He cites two main reasons for this failure.

2. Dreher, *Benedict Option*, 8.
3. Dreher, *Benedict Option*, 12.
4. Dreher, *Benedict Option*, 18.
5. Carrón, *Disarming Beauty*, 7.
6. Carrón, *Disarming Beauty*, 57.

First, the kind of Christianity that was presented was often reduced to an idea, "more notional than real: a set of concepts without reference to concrete life."[7] The theology and even terminology used to express the meaning of Christianity was removed from the person of Christ and relationship with him. When this occurs, Christian faith devolves into a collection of abstract concepts. Second, Christianity is too often reduced to a set of ethics, values, and rules, with the person of Jesus becoming just another historic figure who lived a moral life. Carrón argues that these two bastardized versions of Christianity would not have inspired people to change their lives and follow Christ 2,000 years ago, or at the time of the Reformation, and they are not sufficient today.[8]

Despite past problems with Christian engagement with the world, Carrón is optimistic it can be a transformative power today. He calls for Christians to "communicate the radical novelty of Christianity."[9] This kind of encounter has the power to reawaken a person, to discover her true nature and purpose in life, and leads to a sense of fulfillment. Witnessing in the world today should not start with the presentation of rules, waging of the culture war, or anything approaching heavy-handed indoctrination. Instead, it is the demonstration of how joyful and fulfilling one's life can be after an encounter with Christ.

Where is Merton on this spectrum? He is abundantly clear that Christians should not reflexively reject and turn away from secular culture. Instead, we should look for the good in it, for those things that are valuable to Christ. Merton states that "if we look at the modern world and say 'there is nothing valuable in this mess to Christ . . . in the long run we are going to prove that we are not with Christ because He does see in the modern world something worth dying for . . . There are things in the world which our Lord valued so much that he died on the cross to save them."[10] Merton writes that Christians should approach the world with humility and should not presume that our faith makes us superior to others or entitles us to judge them and decide what is best.

In addition, Merton points out that Christians all too often view the secular world as something that must be confronted and conquered before they will fully live in it. However, he is clear that Christians should accept

---

7. Carrón, *Disarming Beauty*, 60.
8. Carrón, *Disarming Beauty*, 63.
9. Carrón, *Disarming Beauty*, xix.
10. Merton, "Christian in the World," 9:00–10:04.

it on its own terms. As Merton states, "I accept the atheist as atheist. I do not demand that he stop being an atheist or potentially reject his atheism before I will talk to him."[11] He affirms that we should not act as if those who believe differently need to be rescued.[12] As he puts it, "our job is to struggle along with everybody else and collaborate with them in the difficult, frustrating task of seeking a solution to common problems."[13]

In order to do this, Merton calls Christians to engage with others, especially those with whom they differ, to start an open and honest dialogue. While that is the goal, he points out that in practice this often does not happen. Instead, we fail to have a genuine encounter because we have already reduced the other person to a category, e.g., conservative or liberal, Christian or atheist, Boomer or iGen, etc., and assume we already know what the other person thinks or will say about a particular issue. In these cases there is no real exchange of ideas. Instead there is a pretense of conversation in which we are merely biding our time, waiting to employ our ready-made response and talking points to what we expect to hear. As Merton writes, "so many of our responses to the world are simply mechanical and aren't really responses at all, therefore they're dishonest."[14] This failure to genuinely engage with others is also attributable to the fact that we often love our own ideology and opinions more than our desire to serve and love our neighbor. Instead, we seek to glorify our own ideas and the institutions that promote those worldviews rather than authentically communicating with others.[15]

Being a part of the world and fully engaging with it does not mean that Christians should abandon their principles and accept all secular values. Merton calls us to search for and affirm those things in the world that Christ valued. In addition, we should look for parts of popular culture that can be oriented towards our Christian values. For example, he cites the emphasis on accumulating wealth, saying that in and of itself it is not an evil, "There are in the world these immense resources which could be used in which the world is proud of."[16] These can be used for good, e.g., helping those in need, funding organizations working for social change, etc.

---

11. Merton, "Christian in the World," 33:25–33:38.
12. Merton, "Christian in the World," 9:25–9:28.
13. Merton, *Faith and Violence,* 142.
14. Merton, "Christian in the World," 14:36–14:43.
15. Merton, *Faith and Violence,* 162.
16. Merton, "Christian in the World," 24:32–24:37.

Merton acknowledges that engagement with the secular world can be uncomfortable because it faces so many complex problems. As a result, we often avoid difficult and complicated issues because they make us confront an unsettling reality or problem that has no easy solution. He points to racial inequality as an example, stating that many simply respond that "this is a very disturbing nasty mess. Well maybe it's just a distraction. Maybe I'll just keep my peace and forget about it. I can't do anything about it anyway so let's just forget it."[17] Merton is clear that Christians must face the difficult issues and avoid convenient or overly simplistic solutions. We must be prepared to get comfortable with the uncomfortable. As he puts it:

> it would be a most important thing, in the Christian's reaction to the world today, of having to face anguished decisions over a period of time, of not being able to get a decent answer for a long period of time. I would say it's most important that we should not regard this as distracting. We may have to be in positions where there are long periods where our peace is disturbed because we don't know the answer and we are trying to find the answer and we can't find it, and we have to struggle to make up our minds, and we can't make them up. And it would be so nice if we could make up our minds and forget the whole thing and go pray nice and quiet. And we can't. It is a dishonest solution simply to reject this in order to have peace. We must not do this. We are not allowed to do this as Christians.[18]

Confronting these issues is much more important than our own peace of mind. Merton goes on to say that if our response to the world is based on truth it must be informed by genuine knowledge. Therefore, we should remain intellectually curious, endeavoring to stay well informed.

Finally, in addition to affirming the good in secular society and engaging with it, Christians and the church should provide a viable alternative to the one offered by popular culture. This alternative needs to be one of vitality and substance and not presented as some kind of feel-good life hack, marketed like any other self-help product or program. As Merton puts it, "if religion is advertised as a happiness pill, and then a real happiness pill comes along, then I see no justification for religious people complaining that the public likes the competitor's product better."[19]

---

17. Merton, "Christian in the World," 18:47–18:57.
18. Merton, "Christian in the World," 19:12–20:07.
19. Merton, *Faith and Violence*, 217.

Merton and the Individual Witness, Part I

Be in a Faith Community

In looking at Merton's life and writings for guidance one sees the importance of being a part of a faith community. He was constantly looking for ways to get closer to God, but it was always within the context of a religious group. For example, while in India, not long before he died, Merton gave a conference about prayer to a group of Catholic priests and nuns. In the course of his remarks, he discussed the growth of global Communism that was still on the rise in 1968, and offered hope for Christians in a world whose religious institutions were in decline. Merton declared:

> Even if everything else goes, even if Communism takes the world over and closes all your schools and institutions and makes you live in the world without a religious habit as a secular person, if you have your faith and if you are united with others who have the same faith, in love and trust, if there is a Christian community there of some sort you have everything. Nothing can take it away. Nobody can take away from you what you really need, but you have to develop it yourself, with God's grace. You have to work at it.[20]

Merton is clear in his writings and talks that being rooted in a community is a vital part of being Christian. However, a look at his life shows that finding perfect contentment in one can often be a challenge.

Merton and the Quest to Find Home

Someone who only read Merton's autobiography, *The Seven Storey Mountain*, might have the impression that he quickly adjusted to monastic life and contentedly lived out the rest of his days in the woods of Kentucky. That is far from the case, as Merton constantly questioned where he belonged. He considered joining other monastic orders before choosing the Trappists and he continued to do that throughout his life. In his autobiography Merton describes that while researching the Trappist order he came across information about other monastic groups, the Carthusians and Camaldolese, that captured his imagination. The following passage shows his romanticized account of life in one of these orders:

---

20. Merton, "Two Conferences on Prayer," 31:22.

> What I saw on those pages pierced me to the heart like a knife.
>
> What wonderful happiness there was, then, in the world! There were still men on this miserable, noisy, cruel earth, who tasted the marvelous joy of silence and solitude, who dwelt in forgotten mountain cells, in secluded monasteries, where the news and desires and appetites and conflicts of the world no longer reached them.
>
> They were free from the burden of the flesh's tyranny, and their clear vision, clean of the world's smoke and of its bitter sting, were raised to heaven and penetrated into the deeps of heaven's infinite and healing light.
>
> I had to slam the book shut on the picture of Camaldoli and the bearded hermits standing in the stone street of cells, and I went out of the library, trying to stamp out the embers that had broken into flame, there, for an instant, within me.[21]

Later in *The Seven Storey Mountain* Merton describes how happy he would have been to join the Carthusians. However, that was next to impossible since they had no American monasteries at that time and travel to Europe was limited because of the war.[22]

Not long after settling into life at Gethsemani, Merton began to wonder if it would be better to move to another order where he could have more solitude. Once again, he felt the allure of the Carthusians. Merton chronicles much of this questioning in his published journal, *The Sign of Jonas*. During this time, he came to believe that he could best live out his vocation elsewhere, and he challenged his superiors to grant permission to move. These requests were denied.

As Merton accepted the fact that he would not be allowed to become a Carthusian he turned his sights to the Camadolese order and began exploring the possibility of moving to Italy to join them. He wrote Dom Aselmo Giabani, prior of the monastery of Camaldli and prior general of the Camadolse order, declaring that "I am convinced that your life would perfectly suit me."[23]

Merton made official requests to transfer to the Camadolse but was denied. He did not, however, passively accept this refusal as the last word. He corresponded frequently with those inside and outside that order, making the case for his transfer. On at least one occasion Merton's efforts

---

21. Merton, *Seven Storey Mountain*, 346–48.
22. Merton, *Seven Storey Mountain*, 365.
23. Grayston, *Thomas Merton and the Noonday Demon*, 70.

involved an element of spycraft. His incoming mail was screened by his abbot, Dom James Fox. Merton wrote Dom Giabbini, that "Dom James will be back in a few days. If you write me, don't say anything about the matter, even in Italian. But if you want to tell me that you have taken steps to obtain the *transitus* (permission to transfer from one order to another), tell me something like 'We have planted the roses at the hermitage.' And if you have obtained the *transitus*, tell me that 'The roses are *in bloom* at the hermitage.'"[24]

Despite his best efforts, Merton was once again denied permission to leave, and in the spring of 1956, he finally acknowledged that a move to Italy was impossible. Writing once again to the head of the Camaldoli order he conceded that "Our project of last year has completely failed, as you know . . . I have *let go* of the hope of [receiving] a transitus to Camaldoli, and I remain entirely in the hands and at the *disposal* of my good *superiors*."[25] Merton's restlessness, however, soon prompted him to consider yet another move, this time to Central America.

Merton continued to feel restless and sought more solitude and simplicity. He believed Gethsamani had changed significantly and become too crowded and industrialized, ironically in part because of the influx of men who flocked there after reading Merton's writings. In late 1957, poet Ernesto Cardenal, ten years Merton's junior, came to Gethsamani as a novice monk. At that time Merton served as Master of Novices, providing instruction to them. Merton saw Cardenal as a kindred spirit and the two developed a friendship.[26] Over the next two years they hatched a plan to form a new monastic order somewhere in Nicaragua. Cardenal left Gethsemani in 1959 to enter the seminary of *Santa María de la Resurrección* in Cuernavaca, Mexico, and they continued to plan the formation of a new monastic community via correspondence.[27]

Later that year Merton decided he would join Cardenal at the monastery in Mexico and form their new community after Cardenal's formation was completed. In the fall of 1959, the prior of this Benedictine monastery told Merton that church authorities in Rome would allow him to move there. While he was elated, Merton also dreaded telling his Trappist

---

24. Grayston, *Thomas Merton and the Noonday Demon*, 114.
25. Grayston, *Thomas Merton and the Noonday Demon*, 160.
26. Merton and Cardenal, *From the Monastery to the World*, 25.
27. The book *From the Monastery to the World: The Letters of Thomas Merton and Ernesto Cardenal*, edited by Jessie Sandoval, contains all of this correspondence.

superiors and their inevitable resistance to his latest plan to leave Gethsemani. Merton was, however, optimistic that this time he would finally be allowed to move and excitedly began making plans, writing Cardenal to discuss possible locations for their community and ways it should operate. Merton was aware of his "celebrity" status, at least in Catholic circles, and the impact his publicized departure from Gethsemani could have. Towards that end he wrote to Cardenal that they should be measured in sharing details of their plan with the public:

> Because it is very important that no publicity be given to the fact that I have left Gethsemani and the Order, but that even those who know about it should understand it simply as a normal leave of absence. Later when the new venture begins, it will make itself understood on its own terms. Above all nothing must be said about new or special projects, and the worst thing that could happen would be for me to be surrounded by eager inquirers and prospective postulants ready to join a "new Order." That would be fatal.[28]

All of this planning came to an abrupt halt in November 1959. The superiors of Merton's order learned of his plans and summoned Dom James Fox to Rome to meet with them. Shortly after Fox returned to Gethsemani Merton's worst fears were confirmed when he was once again denied permission to leave. In a December 1959 letter to Cardenal, Merton lays the blame for this latest refusal at the feet of noted psychiatrist Dr. Gregory Zilboorg. Merton met with him at a conference in 1956, and Zilboorg had provided a psychological assessment to Merton's superiors. According to Merton, Zilboorg believed his desire for solitude and change was attributable to getting "out from under obedience and that if I were allowed a little liberty I would probably run away with a woman."[29] While still restless, Merton took this latest disappointment in stride, writing to Cardenal that "I can only obey the Congregation and remain passive and I have no hope of making any move to leave this Order. I have in fact promised not to leave, but will only await the action of the Church to move me elsewhere if she sees fit."[30]

Cardenal went on to have an eventful life. In 1979, he joined the Sandinista Revolution that overthrew the Somoza government, eventually serving as the country's Minister of Culture. In 1983, Pope John Paul II publicly

---

28. Merton and Cardenal, *From the Monastery to the World*, 79–80.
29. Merton and Cardenal, *From the Monastery to the World*, 94.
30. Merton and Cardenal, *From the Monastery to the World*, 95.

scolded him on an airport tarmac for ignoring the Pontiff's order to resign from government service and a year later Cardenal was suspended from performing his priestly duties. In 2014, Pope Francis lifted the suspension and reinstated Cardenal into the priesthood. Years after their time together Cardenal looked back fondly on his friendship with Merton, writing "he taught me to be like him, for whom spiritual life was not separate from any other human concern (racism, politics, literature, the nuclear question, etc.) Naturally, we had huge things in common outside the walls of the monastery."[31]

Resigned to stay at Gethsemani, Merton continued to seek more solitude. His abbot finally relented, allowing Merton to live in a hermitage on the monastery grounds. A few entries from Merton's journals during this time illustrate the sense of excitement and peace he felt there. An entry from late September 1963 reflects this: "Yesterday went up to the hermitage and sat on the grass and in the tall trees. The house quiet and cool. A few birds. And nothing. Who would want to live in any other way?"[32] Merton was allowed to spend more time at the hermitage and in October 1964 was allowed to spend the night there for the first time. As his journal indicates, the experience lived up to his expectations:

> Got up there about nightfall. Wonderful silence, saying Compline gently and slowly with a candle burning before the icon of Our Lady. A deep sense of peace and truth. That this was the way things are supposed to be, that I was in my right mind for a change . . . Total absence of care and agitation. Slept wonderfully well . . . I felt very much alive, and real, and awake, surrounded by silence and penetrated by truth.[33]

Finally, late in the summer of 1965, Dom James granted Merton permission to live full-time at the hermitage. His official first day as a hermit was August 20, 1965.[34] After spending time there, Merton wrote about how this place seemed to finally be the right fit for him:

> Everything about this hermitage simply fills me with joy . . . it is the place God has given me after so much prayer and longing— but without my deserving it—and it is a delight. I can imagine no other joy on earth than to have such a place and to be at peace in,

---

31. Merton and Cardenal, *From the Monastery to the World*, 28.
32. Merton, *Dancing in the Water of Life*, 5:20.
33. Merton, *Dancing in the Water of Life*, 5:154.
34. Merton, *Dancing in the Water of Life*, 5:xiv.

> to live in silence, to think and write, to listen to the wind and to all the voices of the wood, to live in the shadow of the big cedar cross, to prepare for my death and my exodus to the heavenly country, to love my brothers and all people, and to pray for the whole world and for peace and good sense among men. So it is "my place" in the scheme of things, and that is sufficient![35]

Merton finally attained the change and solitude that he had sought for so long. However, despite his initial enthusiasm about life at the hermitage, Merton could not escape himself. He soon started giving voice to the need for yet more change. As was discussed in the last chapter, change did indeed come when a new abbot granted permission for Merton to travel to Asia for a conference. While abroad, a month before he died, he reflected on his restlessness and thoughts about his home at Gethsemani. He wrote in his journal:

> Though I fully appreciate the many advantages of the hermitage at Gethsemani, I still have the feeling that the lack of quiet and the general turbulence there, external and internal, last summer are indications that I ought to move. And so far the best indications seem to point to Alaska or to the area around the Redwoods. Another question: would this move be temporary or permanent? I do not think I ought to separate myself completely from Gethsemani, even while maintaining an official residence there, legally only. I suppose I ought eventually to end my days there. I do in many ways miss it. There is no problem of my wanting simply to "leave Gethsemani." It is my monastery and being away has helped me see it in perspective and love it more.[36]

Merton's search for home finally came to an end with his accidental death in Thailand in late 1968.

What We Can Learn from Merton about Community

Many of us that are a part of a faith community sometimes feel unsettled or long for change. It is easy then to relate to Merton's restlessness and feeling that the grass is greener on the other side. His persistent searching, even after being granted more solitude in his hermitage, is also instructive for us because it shows that while change can sometimes bring renewal and

---

35. Merton, *Dancing in the Water of Life*, 5:209.
36. Merton, *Dancing in the Water of Life*, 5:282.

a fresh perspective, it is not a panacea. A perfect community doesn't exist. Any group that allows human beings to join, which is to say every group of every kind, will have the kinds of problems that arise when people come together, e.g., jealousy, pettiness, hypocrisy, abuses of power, etc. Merton dealt with all of those interpersonal dynamics while living at Gethsemani, most notably seen in the complicated relationship with his abbot. He also famously declared that he had no desire to be abbot of his order because he was not able to deal with the "trivialities" of his "confused and anxiety ridden" brother monks[37] While Merton sometimes expressed his frustration about his current situation and longed for a change, he did not walk away from his life as a committed Catholic priest and monk.

Despite all of his questioning, searching, and feelings of restlessness, Merton never chose to go it alone, seeking God solely on his own terms. He made the decision to stay in a group, with all the good and bad that comes along with it. As brilliant as Merton was, he placed himself in a community, acknowledging that the thoughts, opinions, and theological propositions of others carried weight and should be taken seriously.

Following Merton's example means we should seek out a faith community of like-minded believers—Merton was not a None. He shows us that we do not abandon our own individuality, ability to reason, and right to question those things with which we disagree because we are a part of a group. There will inevitably be beliefs and practices that we question or are less committed to than others. This was certainly the case for Merton, and he worked to bring about changes to monasticism. He wrote and spoke to fellow religious about the need for real monastic reform, and not just cosmetic changes to its hierarchical structure, ceremonies, or ways of operating.[38] Specifically, Merton called for monastic orders to be more aware of, and open to, problems in the world, especially the plight of the poor in their surrounding communities. He also cited a need for better ongoing education of its members and called for more authentic communication between them.[39] Following Merton in this way means acting to make any needed changes from within, working to be a part of the solution, rather than standing on the outside, lobbing criticisms at those doing the hard work of change.

---

37. Mott, *Seven Mountains of Thomas Merton*, 503–4.
38. Merton, "Monk in the Diaspora," 300.
39. Merton, *Contemplation in a World of Action*, 136–39.

Being in a faith community should not only nourish and cultivate our faith but it should challenge us as well. Merton understood that living the Christian faith is often inconvenient and at odds with many of the goals and values of our secular, hyper-consumptive society. The faith community we choose should reflect that, offering both support and challenge.

Of course, because of technology, what it means to be a community has changed. The COVID-19 lockdowns certainly brought this issue into focus as in-person worship had to move to virtual options. We should, therefore, be open to new ways of joining others to practice our faith. However, truly being part of a community requires us to do more than just "like" or comment on a Facebook page. Merton shows us that an integral part of being in a community is the acceptance that our own opinions are not the only, or highest, authority on spiritual matters.

Join in the Suffering of Others to Work for Change

Merton was clear that as Christians we are called to oppose evil wherever it is found. We should join in the suffering of others to offer comfort, and more importantly, work to change the conditions that caused that suffering. As he writes, "If evil comes into our life, it is in order that we may grow and give glory to God by cooperating with him in resisting it."[40] Merton did not believe that God is absent from our lives when we face evil and suffering. Instead, he believed that Christ is especially present to us when we suffer.[41] For example, in his book *No Man Is an Island,* Merton writes:

> We all live together in the power of His death which overcame death. We neither suffer alone nor conquer alone nor go off into eternity alone. In Him we are inseparable: therefore, we are free to be fruitfully alone whenever we please, because wherever we go, whatever we suffer, whatever happens to us, we are united with those we love in Him because we are united with Him.[42]

Merton argues that Christians too often focus on their own interior spirituality rather than taking action to oppose injustice. He points to all of the atrocities committed by dictatorships in the twentieth century as proof

---

40. Merton, *Love and Living,* 180

41. For a detailed examination of Merton's thoughts about evil and suffering, and how they were ultimately impacted by his immersion in Zen, see my book *Thomas Merton—Evil and Why We Suffer: From Purified Soul Theodicy to Zen.*

42. Merton, *No Man is an Island,* 86–87.

of that.[43] However, Christian charity should compel a genuine concern for others and an eagerness to work for change. Merton argues that too many Christians mistakenly take this notion of Christian charity simply as a call to be kind to others. This fails to capture the essence of true charity because it focuses our attention on our closest neighbors, which for many middle-class Christians share a lifestyle of "advantages and comforts." As a result we ignore those most in need, "those who are unfortunate, who suffer, who are poor, destitute, or who have nothing in this world . . . "[44]

Merton is clear that charity is more than just prayer, good intentions, or a cheerful attitude. It is meaningless without concrete acts to work for the good of others. He writes that Christians are not worthy of that name unless they give generously of both time and treasure. In addition, our sacrifice to help others must be real and not just some token gesture, which mainly serves to inflate our own ego. Merton declares that token gestures, no matter how well intentioned, can actually be counterproductive as they only treat the surface issues and do nothing to address the root causes of suffering.

Merton also argues that Christians should not dismiss the plight of those suffering from poverty and injustice by concluding it must be the will of God. Instead, those conditions are caused by very human "incompetence, injustice, and the economic and social confusion of our rapidly developing world."[45] Finally, Merton is clear that the enormity of suffering in the world should not deter Christians from trying to make changes. No one individual can fix all of the world's problems, but he writes that "one should know when one can do something to help alleviate suffering and poverty, and realize when one is implicitly cooperating in evils which prolong or intensify suffering and poverty. In other words, Christian charity is no longer real unless it is accompanied by a concern with social justice."[46]

The Fight for Racial Justice

Merton's efforts to join with others to oppose evil and alleviate suffering is perhaps best seen in his writings about race. He was greatly troubled by the plight of African Americans and supported their struggle for equality.

---

43. Merton, *Life and Holiness*, 20.
44. Merton, *Life and Holiness*, 88.
45. Merton, *Life and Holiness*, 90.
46. Merton, *Life and Holiness*, 90.

Towards that end he lent his voice to that cause and, beginning in the early 1960s, he dedicated a number of essays and articles to the topic. Merton believed our society had reached a providential moment for both black and white Americans. He writes that this is

> the moment in which, hearing and understanding the will of God as expressed in the urgent need of our Negro brother, we can respond to that inscrutable will in a faith that faces the need of reform and creative change, in order that the demands of truth and justice may not go unfulfilled. It is a moment of freedom and salvation for both races.[47]

There are three prophetic elements of Merton's writings that make them so relevant today.[48] First, Merton points to racism within the Christian community that perpetuates the problem. Second, he calls out the large number of whites who are sympathetic to the call for racial equality but fail to act for real change, instead opting for the comfort of the status quo. Finally, Merton calls attention to the reality of structural, systemic racism. I will use these categories to frame Merton's writings about race.

Christian Complicity

Merton does not shy away from acknowledging that Christians have been directly and indirectly complicit in perpetuating racism. Acts of racism and violence underscore the chasm between what is preached and what is practiced by some Christians. For example, in Pope Paul IV's opening statement to a session of the Second Vatican Council, he urged Christians to manifest Christ in the world. However, not long after the pontiff made those remarks some Catholics in Louisiana set fire to their own parochial school to prevent it from being integrated. Around the same time in another parish, a priest was beaten by his own congregants for the unpardonable offense of giving communion to white and black children at the same time.[49] Professed Christians who commit racial violence fail to see Christ in African Americans. As Merton bluntly puts it, if they did "it would not be easy for a Christian to mutilate another man, string him up on a tree

---

47. Merton, *Seeds of Destruction*, 65.

48. Theologian and Merton scholar Dan Horan makes a similar point ("Thomas Merton & Black Lives Matter").

49. Merton, *Seeds of Destruction*, 12.

and shoot him full of holes if he believed that what he did to that man was done to Christ."[50]

Merton also notes that many white Christians indirectly contribute to the problem of racism by only making some kind of token gesture or parroting some trite slogan about the need for "brotherly love." These ineffectual actions lead many to believe they've done their part to address racism and "have then taken as a total dispensation from all meaningful action and genuine concern in the crucial problems of our time. As a result, they have become unable to listen to the voice of God in the events of the time, and have resisted that voice instead of obeying it."[51]

Merton also challenges many white Christians who seek to downplay the issue of racial inequality by pointing to new laws that were passed to ensure fair treatment for all. He writes:

> Here I can see you will protest. You will point to the Supreme Court decisions that have upheld Negro rights, to education in integrated colleges and schools. It seems to me that our motives are judged by the real fruit of our decisions. What have we done? We have been willing to grant the Negro rights on paper, even in the South. But the laws have been framed in such a way that in every case their execution has depended on the good will of white society, and the white man has not failed, when left to himself, to block, obstruct, or simply forget the necessary action without which the rights of the Negro cannot be enjoyed in fact.[52]

Most of Merton's writings about race came after the passage of the 1964 Civil Rights Act. He recognized that the passage of that legislation was merely the start of a new phase and struggle against discrimination—not the solution.[53]

Merton also acknowledges that some white Christians argue racism is no longer a problem and point to selective statistics that show rising income levels for African Americans. He writes that this kind of argument appeals to the ideals of our own consumeristic culture, in which accumulating and spending money is the highest goal, and "should satisfy the mind of anyone who believes in money."[54]

---

50. Merton, *Seeds of Destruction*, 17.
51. Merton, *Seeds of Destruction*, 88.
52. Merton, *Seeds of Destruction*, 18.
53. Merton, *Seeds of Destruction*, 85.
54. Merton, *Seeds of Destruction*, 26.

Preservation of the Status Quo

In one of Merton's most famous essays about race, "Letters to a White Liberal," he takes aim at white progressives who, on the surface, express sympathy for the plight of African Americans but fail to act to make any meaningful changes. The following long passage shows his directness in speaking to them:

> Now, my liberal friend, here is your situation. You, the well-meaning liberal, are right in the middle of all this confusion. You are, in fact, a political catalyst. On the one hand, with your good will and your ideals, your fine hopes and your generous, but vague, love of mankind in the abstract and of rights enthroned on a juridical Olympus, you offer a certain encouragement to the Negro (and you do right, my only complaint being that you are not yet right enough) so that, abetted by you, he is emboldened to demand concessions. Though he knows you will not support all his demands, he is well aware that you will be forced to support some of them in order to maintain your image of yourself as a liberal. He also knows, however, that your material comforts, your security, and your congenial relations with the establishment are much more important to you than your rather volatile idealism, and that when the game gets rough you will be quick to see your own interests menaced by his demands. And you will sell him down the river for the five hundredth time in order to protect yourself. For this reason, as well as to support your own self-esteem, you are very anxious to have a position of leadership and control in the Negro's fight for rights, in order to be able to apply the brakes when you feel it is necessary.[55]

Merton is clear that transformative societal change will not happen as long as parts of white society cling to the status quo. Changes to our social and economic system would be disruptive, and that is something that, "even for those white liberals who gather for marches and chant the right slogans, is unacceptable." As he writes:

> The problem is this: if the Negro, as he actually is . . . enters wholly into white society, then that society is going to be radically changed . . . The tempo of life and its tone will be altered. The face of business and professional life may change. The approach to the

---

55. Merton, *Seeds of Destruction*, 33.

coming crucial labor and economic problems will be even more anguished than we have feared.[56]

Merton believes that too many whites are willing to ignore the plight of blacks because taking it seriously would disrupt their own peace of mind and material comfort. This leads them to treat African Americans as if they are invisible, refusing to let them take shape as full people, "lest he demand the treatment due to a human person and a free citizen of this nation."[57] Merton argues that this is one of the factors that prompts demonstrations. Public protests are one tangible way for African Americans to make themselves visible to the white ruling class, and in this way can "finally disturb the white man's precious 'peace of soul.'"[58]

Merton writes that this is the reason so many whites are uneasy about black protests—because they are a challenge to their own comfort and status. A true and deep encounter with those calling for change would force these whites to admit their prosperity is to some extent rooted in the system that perpetuates this injustice. It follows then that this could possibly lead to "a complete re-examination of the political motives behind all our current policies, domestic and foreign, with the possible admission that we are wrong."[59] This challenge to the status quo also makes many white people defensive. This ultimately leads them to ignore their pangs of conscience in favor of "their taste for compromise, their desire to eat momma's cherry pie and still have it, their semi-conscious proclivity to use the Negro for their own sentimental, self-justifying ends."[60] Merton reaffirms his belief that these liberals ultimately choose the preservation of the status quo, and side with institutions that will perpetuate those conditions, rather than make the structural reforms needed to produce real changes.

Merton also addressed the rise of the Black Power movement and its, as he characterized it, more aggressive tactics to demand change. This led some whites, who were already eager to dismiss the movement for equal rights, to claim outside forces had co-opted it in an effort to sow national discontent. Merton writes they saw these efforts "as an obviously sinister cloak for Communist machinations. It has to be unmasked as pure malevolence, so that the appeal it aims at the white conscience may be discredited

---

56. Merton, *Seeds of Destruction*, 8.
57. Merton, *Seeds of Destruction*, 21.
58. Merton, *Seeds of Destruction*, 21.
59. Merton, *Seeds of Destruction*, 48.
60. Merton, *Faith and Violence*, 124.

and ignored."[61] Merton believed that the emergence of the Black Power movement was just what many white Americans secretly wanted. That is, it allowed these whites to dismiss the entire call for equal rights as radical and something that should be opposed in order to preserve peace. As he describes, it made many "deliciously afraid. And glad. Because now things were so much simpler. One had perfectly good reasons to call out the cops and the National Guard."[62]

Systemic Racism

Finally, in the essay "The Hot Summer of Sixty-Seven," written near the end of his life, Merton reflects on some of his previous writings on race, especially "Letters to a White Liberal." He noted that a number of readers objected to the notion that they were somehow to blame for the racial injustice of that time. After all, they hadn't personally discriminated against or mistreated anyone and didn't believe they deserved to be lumped in with those who had. In addition, they also rejected the idea that they should admit some kind of complicity in order to deal with the problem of racial inequality. However, Merton pointed to the reality of systemic racism that unavoidably included the entire white race. The following long passage encapsulated Merton's thoughts on this issue:

> There is, however, such a thing as collective responsibility, and collective guilt. This is not quite the same as personal responsibility and personal guilt, because it does not usually follow from a direct fully conscious act of choice. Few of us have actively and consciously chosen to oppress and mistreat the Negro. But nevertheless we have all more or less acquiesced in and consented to a state of affairs in which the Negro is treated unjustly, and in which his unjust treatment is directly or indirectly to the advantage of people like ourselves, people with whom we agree and collaborate, people with whom we are in fact identified. So that even if in theory the white man may believe himself to be well disposed toward the Negro—and never gets into a bind in which he proves himself to be otherwise—we all collectively contribute to a situation in which the Negro has to live and act as our inferior. I am personally convinced that most white people who think themselves very "fair" to the Negro show, by the way they imagine themselves "fair," that

---

61. Merton, *Seeds of Destruction*, 51.
62. Merton, *Faith and Violence*, 122.

they consider the Negro an inferior type of human being, a sort of "minor," and their "fairness" consists in giving him certain benefits provided he "keeps in his place," the place they have allocated to him as an inferior. I would like to say that this state of mind is itself an act of inhumanity and injustice against the Negro and is in fact at the root of the trouble with the Negro, so that anyone who holds such opinions, even in the best of faith, is contributing actively to the violence of the present situation whether he realizes it or not.[63]

Merton argues that too many whites believe that African Americans are trying to be "accepted" into white society or absorbed by it. This kind of thinking only perpetuates the problem of systemic racism because it sets whiteness as the norm or ideal to aspire to. As Merton writes:

> The actions and attitudes of white Christians all, without exception, contain a basic and axiomatic assumption of white superiority, even when the pleas of the Negro for equal rights are hailed with the greatest benevolence. It is simply taken for granted that, since the white man is superior, the Negro wants to become a white man. And we, liberals and Christians that we are, advance generously, with open arms, to embrace our little black brother and welcome him into white society.[64]

Merton writes that a genuinely Christian attitude about race is one that recognizes and accepts the fact that different races and cultures are correlative. That is, they complete one another, with the white race needing the black race and the black race needing the white one.[65]

Merton also contends that the ruling class should not be surprised when these inequities produce demonstrations from groups discriminated against: "If you are knowingly responsible for laws that will be systematically violated, then you are partly to blame for the disorders and the confusion resulting from civil disobedience and even revolution."[66] He goes on to write that one of the purposes of nonviolent protests is to awaken the conscience of white society to the reality of injustice and its complicity in creating this situation. In this way Merton hopes that white Americans will grasp that the "black problem" is actually a "white problem" and "that the cancer of injustice and hate which is eating white society . . . is rooted in the

---

63. Merton, *Faith and Violence*, 180.
64. Merton, *Seeds of Destruction*, 58.
65. Merton, *Seeds of Destruction*, 61.
66. Merton, *Seeds of Destruction*, 20.

heart of the white man himself."[67] Merton recognizes that this problem is complex and cannot easily or quickly be fixed, and he does not provide any facile answers. However, he does suggest that we start with the recognition that the problem exists and honestly confront it in order to continue the slow process of change.

Merton and Working for Change

Merton did not just identify inequality, he worked to do something about it. For him, it was writing and speaking out about the problem, with a focus on its root causes. Merton shows us that we must genuinely recognize others as being fully human, and ultimately see Christ in them, if we are going to join with them to stop the conditions that cause suffering. To do this we need to resist the instinct to be dismissive of those who are different than us. However, we must be prepared to encounter life experiences that are different from our own, and not reject them because they are not like ours.

In working for change we should focus on those things that are within our scope of influence. In addition, we should also do everything possible to focus on the sources that produce inequality and suffering. This involves giving of our time and resources, locally and nationally, and joining with others to fight injustice. This work will be slow, often frustrating, and will challenge our own love of comfort and peace of mind, i.e., the status quo. However, as Merton shows, as Christians, that is what we are called to do.

---

67. Merton, *Seeds of Destruction*, 45.

5

Merton and the Individual Witness, Part II

Work for Peace

Living in the Shadow of War

Thomas Merton was an influential voice for peace. As Gordon C. Zahn writes, Merton was not the first or only prominent Catholic to write about nonviolence, "but he did succeed better than any other in bringing it to the attention of an American audience."[1] The specter of war cast a long shadow over Merton's entire life. Born in 1915, he entered a world engulfed by it. Merton's parents uprooted their lives and fled France for the safety of the United States just months after Thomas was born. Merton chose to begin his autobiography by juxtaposing his birth with that of a world ravaged by war and death. As he writes:

> On the last day of January 1915, under the sign of the Water Bearer, in a year of a great war, and down in the shadow of some French mountains on the borders of Spain, I came into the world. Free by nature, in the image of God, I was nevertheless the prisoner of my own violence and my own selfishness, in the image of the world into which I was born. That world was the picture of Hell, full of men like myself, loving God and yet hating Him; born to love Him, living instead in fear and hopeless self-contradictory hungers.

1. Zahn, "Original Child Monk," xxviii.

> Not many hundreds of miles away from the house where I was born, they were picking up the men who rotted in the rainy ditches among the dead horses and the ruined seventy-fives, in a forest of trees without branches along the river Marne.[2]

As a young man, war again played a role at a pivotal time, forcing him to decide what to do with his life. After his conversion to Catholicism, Merton was pursuing a career as a novelist, teaching and working on a PhD, and doing volunteer work with the poor in Harlem. During this time he was also trying to discern a call to the priesthood. As was discussed in the previous chapter this deliberation was cut short when it became apparent that he was likely to be drafted. Thus, after some hasty preparations, he headed down to Kentucky to join the Trappists.

Finally, Merton confronted war and the real threat of the total destruction of the human race during the last decade of his life. His writings on peace during this time were greatly influenced by the nuclear arms race. Merton believed that humanity was on the brink of extinction and immediate action was needed to de-escalate the Cold War. In addition, he spoke out in the early days of the war in Vietnam, questioning the United States' motives and tactics, and warned about some of the unintended consequences that could result. Merton reminded Christians that working for peace was an essential part of following Christ, both through prayer and by taking concrete actions.

Merton and Pacifism

Merton was opposed to war and promoted nonviolence, but he was not a pacifist in the sense that he opposed war in every situation. In a journal entry from September 21, 1941, he reflects on the war that was raging and the threat Nazism posed. He writes that "the Germans are putting the whole world in danger of brutal and irresponsible and horrible and maniac policies of government, including slavery and the extermination of religions (ultimately) and a certain amount of 'hygienic' killing of sick or nervous people."[3] To combat this great force had to be used to defeat the evil of Nazism, "hitting the enemy the most dangerous and terrifying

---

2. Merton, *Seven Storey Mountain*, 3.
3. Merton, *Run to the Mountain*, 1:414.

kind of blows you can conceive."[4] He acknowledges the brutality of war and certainty of civilian deaths. However, given the threat the Nazis posed, he asks, "is it charitable to refuse to fight them, or to have anything to do with an army fighting them? Is it loving your neighbor to acquiesce in a bunch of completely unprincipled murderers getting control of the world?"[5]

Merton was willing to serve in the war in a non-combatant role. In a letter he wrote to the draft board in 1941, he declared: "I cannot conceive how killing a man with a flame thrower, a machine gun or a bomb is compatible with a life of Christian perfection along these lines." However, he went on to express his willingness to serve in the military in other capacities:

> [I am willing to serve so long as it involves] no part in the machinery that produces the death of men. Merely being a non-combatant member of a combatant unit is not enough ... I am willing and eager to serve in any post where the work is saving lives and helping those in suffering: ambulance work, hospital work, air raid protection work, etc. I do not ask for any position that would necessarily be remote from the line of fire, or "out of danger."[6]

Merton's qualified pacifism was based on his qualified belief in the just war doctrine. Rooted in the thought of Saint Augustine, the just war theory holds that if a conflict meets certain requirements then it can be considered morally just. Those requirements include the war being fought for good or defensive purposes, waged by legitimate military authority, force is limited to defend and end the conflict, and the lives of noncombatants must be protected.

Merton maintained this stance about war throughout his life. In a letter in late 1961, he was clear that he did not consider himself to be a total pacifist. He affirmed that while Christians should try to practice nonviolence he plainly stated, "I still admit some persons might licitly wage war to defend themselves (for instance the Hungarians in 1956)."[7] In 1966, he gave a conference to his fellow monks about a meeting he had with Vietnamese monk Thich Nhat Hanh and conceded that "sometimes you see there are

---

4. Merton, *Run to the Mountain*, 1:414.
5. Merton, *Run to the Mountain*, 1:414.
6. Forest, *Root of War is Fear*, 9–10.
7. Merton, *Cold War Letters*, 14.

wars that have to be fought and there's nothing you can do to get around them and so forth."[8]

While Merton believed it was still possible for modern conflicts to meet the just war criteria, the technology used in recent conflicts made it increasingly difficult. As he writes, "I agree that even today a just war might theoretically be possible. But I also think we must take into account a totally new situation in which the danger of any war escalating to all out proportions makes it imperative to find other ways of resolving international conflicts. In practice the just war theory has become irrelevant."[9]

Merton also points to the Second World War to show how a conflict could initially meet the criteria for just war, only to have the tactics of modern warfare make them moot. He is clear that initially the Allies were obliged to combat totalitarianism, "with a just cause if ever there was one" and there being "no question about the morality of America's entering the war to defend its rights. Here was a very clear example of a 'just cause' for war."[10] Merton acknowledges that when a nation goes to war the military's goal is to win, and to do so decisively. So, a conflict that begins as a defensive just war often turns into an all-out effort to destroy the enemy, with an ends-justify-the-means mentality: "This will save lives. It is necessary to end the war sooner, and to punish the unjust aggressor."[11]

Nonviolence as an Essential Part of Christian Life

Despite his ambivalent attitude towards the idea of a just war, Merton was a steadfast proponent of nonviolence. He saw it as a cornerstone of being a Christian. We are called to see Christ in everyone we encounter, even when some of those people are "unjust, wicked and odious to us."[12] Christians have an obligation to be patient, and act without hatred, resentment, or hostility towards those who oppose them. Jesus' charge to love our enemies was more than just an aspirational goal, it was a command that requires real action. As Merton writes, "Christ our Lord did not come to bring peace to the world as a kind of spiritual tranquillizer. He brought to His disciples

---

8. Merton, "Thich Nhat Hanh," 30:46–30:50.
9. Merton, *Nonviolent Alternative*, 90.
10. Merton, *Nonviolent Alternative*, 94.
11. Merton, *Nonviolent Alternative*, 97.
12. Merton, *Nonviolent Alternative*, 112.

a vocation and a task, to struggle in the world of violence to establish His peace not only in their hearts but in society itself."[13]

Merton recognized that in practice this can be exceedingly difficult, "especially when the adversary is aroused to a bitter and violent defense of an injustice which he believes to be just."[14] However, that is what is called for, and it often produces better results than those achieved through the use of force. As Merton writes "A non-violent victory, while far more difficult to achieve, stands better chance of curing the illness instead of contracting it." This is because Christian nonviolence seeks to "win" not by destroying or humiliating one's opponent but by "convincing him that there is a higher and more certain common good that can be attained by bombs and blood."[15]

Nuclear War

Merton was categorically opposed to the use of nuclear weapons. In addition, he believed that their use was not just possible but all too probable writing "we are likely to be in a global war within five years . . . and that there is no serious chance of unilateral disarmament."[16] While the situation was dire Merton believed there was still time to prevent Armageddon. He writes, "the end of our civilized society is quite literally up to us and our immediate descendants, if any. It is for us to decide whether we are going to give in to hatred, terror and blind love of power for its own sake, and thus plunge our world in the abyss, or whether restraining our savagery, we can patiently and humanely work together for interests which transcends the limits of any national or ideological community."[17]

Merton criticized those, including Christians, that thought nuclear weapons were a necessary evil needed to keep the peace. In particular, he was frustrated that so many people were willing to overlook the immorality posed by weapons that were capable of indiscriminately killing so many. Merton writes that the use of nuclear weapons, even in defense, was contrary to Christian morality, "I wish to insist above all on one fundamental truth: that all nuclear war, and indeed massive destruction of cities,

---

13. Merton, *Nonviolent Alternative*, 112–13.
14. Merton, *Conjectures of a Guilty Bystander*, 86–87.
15. Merton, *Faith and Violence*, 12.
16. Merton, *Peace in the Post-Christian Era*, 16–17.
17. Merton, *Peace in the Post-Christian Era*, 25.

populations, nations and cultures by any means whatever is a serious crime which is forbidden to us not only by Christian ethics but by every sane and serious moral code."[18] While Merton believed it was theoretically possible for some modern conflicts to be deemed licit under the just war theory, he was clear that any use of nuclear weapons could never be justified. He writes that because of their destructive power and the indiscriminate damage they caused "nuclear war is by its very nature beyond the limits of the traditional doctrine."[19]

Vietnam

Merton was also outspoken in his opposition to the war in Vietnam. He believed that the carnage there was contrary to basic human reason, sanity, justice, and love.[20] In addition, he warned that the war could grow into an even larger global conflict.[21] Finally, Merton did not believe it met the Catholic Church's criteria to be considered just.[22]

Merton was specific in criticizing the ways the United States was waging the war. First, he states that there was a disproportionate number of noncombatants who were being injured and killed. He believed this was largely avoidable and doing so would not harm our war effort. Merton believed these civilian deaths were intended to systematically break the resistance of the North Vietnamese people and government.[23] He also worried these tactics would damage the reputation of the United States throughout the rest of the world. As he writes, "even the most morally insensitive individuals must be able to see that there is something revolting and shameful in the spectacle of the world's greatest superpower smashing with all the force of its most modern weapons into the utterly defenseless villages of a primitive and nonwhite people—and destroying crops into the bargain."[24]

Merton was also worried about the effect our war efforts would have here in the United States. He warned that Americans should not be surprised if "we wake up one day to find fire and violence in our own front

---

18. Merton, *Peace in the Post-Christian Era*, 19.
19. Merton, *Nonviolent Alternative*, 224.
20. Merton, *Nonviolent Alternative*, 263.
21. Merton, "Thich Nhat Hanh," 17:48–17:57.
22. Letter to Jim Forest on July 22, 1964 (Forest, *Root of War is Fear*, 110).
23. Merton, *Nonviolent Alternative*, 265.
24. Merton, *Nonviolent Alternative*, 266.

yards here in America. If the fire of hatred and violent anarchy happens to break out in some of our cities (as it can surely be expected to do sooner or later), we will simply be getting a taste—perhaps only a very slight taste—of our own medicine."[25]

Action

Merton was clear that prayers would not be enough and that Christians had to work for peace. He warned that "it is all too easy to retire into the ivory tower of private spirituality and let the world blow itself to pieces."[26] In addition, no theological argument or spiritual proclamation, no matter how heartfelt or well articulated, will move anyone who "does not already think as we do."[27] Instead, Christians are called to "manifest the truth of the Gospel in social action, with or without explanation. The more clearly his life manifests the teaching of Christ, the more salutary will it be. Clear and decisive Christian action explains itself and teaches in a way that words never can."[28] Indeed, Merton declared that our social actions should demonstrably conform with our religious beliefs and should inform our politics.[29]

It is important to note that Merton did not believe that Christian nonviolence implies any kind of passivity or that it "accepts any kind of disorder, compromises with error and with evil" in order to maintain peace at any price.[30] He affirmed that when attacked an individual has a right and an obligation to protect oneself and family, even to the point of killing the aggressor if that is necessary. Merton writes that failure to oppose evil is "a travesty of Christian meekness. It is purely and simply the sin of cowardice."[31]

Merton identified three essential components of a Christian approach for peace work. First, its goal should be the transformation of the present state of the world, and should not be connected to any political party or system that is abusing its power. Second, those born in a powerful nation,

25. Merton, *Nonviolent Alternative*, 265.
26. Merton, *Nonviolent Alternative*, 79.
27. Merton, *Nonviolent Alternative*, 222.
28. Merton, *Nonviolent Alternative*, 222.
29. Merton, *Nonviolent Alternative*, 223.
30. Merton, *Nonviolent Alternative*, 34–35.
31. Merton, *Nonviolent Alternative*, 104.

or "in some sense a privileged member of world society," should recognize their status and ensure their motives are to help those that are less fortunate and not perpetuate the status quo that enriches them. Finally, the way Christians promote nonviolence is as important as the end result. That is, dishonesty or unethical tactics should be avoided—the ends do not justify the means. Merton is clear that we must also recognize our own inclinations for what we profess to oppose, "our own violence, fanaticism, and greed."[32]

Merton acknowledges that the problem of war seems to be too large for any one person to make a difference. However, he writes that we should focus on those things that we can do in our communities. Merton also warns against the tendency to take refuge in extremism when problems seem too large to handle and one's "political habits and instincts fail to instruct him adequately."[33]

In addition, Merton urged Christians to actively be a part of the political process, researching candidates' positions on important issues and voting for those who share a commitment to peace.[34] However, merely doing one's civic duty of voting is not enough. He also called for Christians to make their voices heard to protest "clearly and forcibly against trends that lead inevitably to crimes which the Church deplores and condemns."[35]

Merton believed that Christians have a special responsibility, informed by their faith, to work for peace, and he thought that Western Christians had failed to lead in these efforts. For example, he called Christians to task for not being more outspoken against the nuclear arms race. He described the prevailing Christian response at that time as being "embarrassed silence, despondent passivity, or crusading belligerence."[36] Merton believed this failure to lead was partly due to the fact that Western Christianity had become aligned with preserving the status quo and "yielding to the hegemony of naked power."[37]

Merton maintained a pragmatic approach to issues of nonviolence. He was clear that peace work must be "realistic and concrete," and, like any

32. Merton, *Nonviolent Alternative*, 22.
33. Merton, *Nonviolent Alternative*, 78.
34. Merton, *Nonviolent Alternative*, 127.
35. Merton, *Nonviolent Alternative*, 127.
36. Merton, *Peace in the Post-Christian Era*, 3.
37. Merton, *Peace in the Post-Christian Era*, 72.

other political strategy, should focus on the "art of the possible."[38] In addition, he also warned that these efforts will take a great deal of time, and, as such, Christians should resist the "fetishism of immediate visible results."[39]

Merton also recognized that a large part of society looked askance at the peace movement of his time. He believed it had an image problem and was dismissed by some as impractical, "an unhealthy kind of idealism," or worse, it was viewed as a tool of Communists to subvert our government. Merton also questioned some of the tactics employed by those actively promoting nonviolence as being either misguided or counterproductive. For example, he believed that some of the peace protests were "harming the peace movement rather than helping it, and that it is in fact fanning up the war rather than abating it."[40]

In urging Christians to do more than just pray and to take action he called for them to protest against nuclear proliferation and align themselves with others who share this commitment to peace. Further, he called for the multilateral disarmament of nuclear weapons. He recognized that tensions were high but thought it was unrealistic to wait for conditions to change.[41] Thus, he called for the creation of an international body with the power to sanction and control the technology and development of nuclear weapons. Merton went on to declare that "a Christian who is not willing to envisage the creation of an effective international authority to control the destinies of man for peace is not acting and thinking as a mature member of the Church."[42] While some Christians may thoughtfully disagree with that particular course of action, everyone should be able to agree on the importance of never using these weapons.

When it came to the conflict in Vietnam, Merton writes that Christians have a moral responsibility to act. Specifically, he urged Christians to do everything they could to help the innocent victims of the war. He suggested that this could be done by sending money to organizations that provided aid for them and taking political action to ensure more was being done to assist these victims. Merton stated that such an effort was in no way

---

38. Merton, *Conjectures of a Guilty Bystander*, 19.
39. Merton, *Conjectures of a Guilty Bystander*, 22.
40. Merton, *Hidden Ground of Love*, 286.
41. Merton, *Peace in the Post-Christian Era*, 17.
42. Merton, *Peace in the Post-Christian Era*, 106.

disloyal to America, and doing so could "salvage a vestige of our Christian decency."[43]

Merton's Struggle to Write about Peace

It is important to note the obstacles Merton had to overcome in order to write about war and peace. Merton dealt with the censorship of his writings from his earliest days in the Trappist order, and it certainly applied to these subjects as well. In the spring of 1962, after publishing the poem "Original Child Bomb" and a heavily censored article about peace, he received word from the head of his order that he was forbidden to publish anything else about these topics. At the time, Merton was keenly focused on these issues and was finishing a book, *Peace in the Post-Christian Era*, that would finally be published decades after he died.

Merton appealed his superior's decision but was denied. He was understandably frustrated, as seen in a letter to Jim Forest, writing that the order's decision

> reflects an astounding incomprehension of the seriousness of the present crisis in its religious aspect ... The reason given is that this is not the right kind of work for a monk, and that it "falsifies the monastic message." Imagine that: the thought that a monk might be deeply enough concerned with the issue of nuclear war to voice a protest against the arms race.[44]

Merton considered this to be particularly rich given the state of monasticism and its reputation at that time. In the same letter to Forest, he writes "Man, I would think that it might just possibly salvage a last thread of repute for an institution that many consider to be dead on its feet. That is really the most absurd aspect of the whole situation, that these people insist on digging their own grave and erecting over it the most monumental kind of tombstone."[45]

In an interesting turn of events his longtime abbot and frenemy Dom James Fox saw a way for Merton to continue expressing his views about peace while complying with the specific instruction not to write about these issues for book publishers. Fox allowed Merton to continue writing,

---

43. Merton, *Nonviolent Alternative*, 266.
44. Forest, *Root of War is Fear*, 55.
45. Forest, *Root of War is Fear*, 55.

with mimeographed copies of his book *Peace in the Post-Christian Era* being sent to friends. In addition, Merton also began writing and distributing a collection of letters about peace that he called *The Cold War Letters*. This allowed Merton to continue sharing his thoughts with a carefully selected public audience.

The Individual Witness and Peacemaking

Many of the larger issues of war and peace Merton confronted are still very much of a concern today. As of this writing, the United States messily ended its twentieth year of war in Afghanistan. Technology has made it much less necessary for the United States to commit troops to a conflict, and, as such, "targeted" missile strikes and bombings have become so common that they often fail to get more than a mention on the nightly news.

Following Merton's example means actively working for peace. For him it was rooted in his Christian faith and a natural part of seeing Christ in others. Merton is clear that quiet acts of piety are not enough. We must take action! This work includes thoughtfully voting for political candidates who share these values and joining with like-minded people whose combined voices have a chance of influencing policy. In addition, we should also contribute time and money to organizations that help those suffering in war-torn areas.

Merton is clear that we should be careful not to take on an ends-justify-the-means mentality. He also warns that our passion for peace should not lead us to reduce those opposed to us to being caricatures, without any humanity. Merton reminds us that we must continue to try to find common ground and areas of agreement, even with enemies.

Finally, it is fitting to give Merton the last word in this section about peace. He wrote the following prayer, read in the House of Representatives on April 12, 1962. It encapsulates Merton's thoughts about war, its root causes, and hope in Christ:

> Almighty and merciful God, Father of all men, Creator and ruler of the universe, Lord of all history, whose designs are without blemish, whose compassion for the errors of men is inexhaustible, in your will is our peace.
> Mercifully hear this prayer which rises to you from the tumult and desperation of a world in which you are forgotten, in which your

name is not invoked, your laws are derided and your presence is ignored. Because we do not know you, we have no peace.

From the heart of an eternal silence, you have watched the rise of empires and have seen the smoke of their downfall. You have seen Egypt, Assyria, Babylon, Greece and Rome, once powerful, carried away like sand in the wind. You have witnessed the impious fury of ten thousand fratricidal wars, in which great powers have torn whole continents to shreds in the name of peace and justice.

And now our nation itself stands in imminent danger of a war the like of which has never been seen! This nation dedicated to freedom, not to power, has obtained, through freedom, a power it did not desire. And seeking by that power to defend its freedom, it is enslaved by the processes and policies of power. Must we wage a war we do not desire, a war that can do no good, and which our very hatred of war forces us to prepare?

A day of ominous decision has now dawned on this free nation. Armed with a titanic weapon, and convinced of our own right, we face a powerful adversary, armed with the same weapon, equally convinced he is right. In this moment of destiny, this moment we never foresaw, we cannot afford to fail. Our choice of peace or war may decide our judgment and publish it in the eternal record. In this fatal moment of choice in which we might begin the patient architecture of peace. We may also take the last step across the rim of chaos.

Save us then from our obsessions! Open our eyes, dissipate our confusions, teach us to understand ourselves and our adversary. Let us never forget that sins against the law of love are punishable by loss of faith, and those without faith stop at no crime to achieve their ends!

Help us to be masters of the weapons that threaten to master us. Help us to use our science for peace and plenty, not for war and destruction. Show us how to use atomic power to bless our children's children, not to blight them. Save us from the compulsion to follow our adversaries in all that we most hate, confirming them in their hatred and suspicion of us. Resolve our inner contradictions, which now grow beyond belief and beyond bearing. They are at once a torment and a blessing: for if you had not left us the light of conscience, we would not have to endure them. Teach us to be long-suffering in anguish and insecurity. Teach us to wait and trust.

Grant light, grant strength and patience to all who work for peace, to this Congress, our President, our military forces, and our adversaries. Grant us prudence in proportion to our power, wisdom in proportion to our science, humaneness in proportion to our wealth and might. And bless our earnest will to help all races and peoples to travel, in friendship with us, along the road to justice, liberty, and lasting peace; But grant us above all to see that our ways are not necessarily your ways, that we cannot fully penetrate the mystery of your designs and that the very storm of power now raging on this earth reveals your hidden will and your inscrutable decision.

Grant us to see your face in the lightning of this cosmic storm, O God of holiness, merciful to men. Grant us to seek peace where it is truly found. In your will, O God, is our peace.
Amen.

Affirm the Truth Wherever It Is Found

Thomas Merton taught us a valuable lesson by actively seeking out and affirming the truth wherever it could be found. As Merton scholar Christopher Pramuk pointed out in a lecture at the 2015 Festival of Faiths, Merton strove to authentically engage others as full human beings and not reduce them to some kind of type or category, e.g., gay/straight, liberal/conservative, etc. Merton did this "in his willingness, over and over again, to open himself completely to an encounter with the other across lines of difference, to be challenged, moved, and changed by the encounter, and from there to critically question and playfully deepen his own tradition's prevailing assumptions, images, and language about God."[46]

Merton developed this kind of openness in the last part of his life. One of the criticisms of his autobiography was its triumphalist stance on Catholicism. At that time Merton was a fresh convert and it shows in his romanticized description of the Catholic Church and casual dismissal of other Christian and world faiths. However, in the last decade and a half of his life Merton actively sought to find common ground with those of other faiths as well as those who had no religious faith or who were critics of Christianity.

It is important to stress that this openness to finding the truth in other religions does not imply that Merton abandoned Catholicism. Instead, he saw it as a way of enhancing his own faith. When it came to

---

46. Festival of Faiths, "Thomas Merton and Race," 19:06–19:28.

exploring other world religions Merton pointed to the teaching of Vatican II. He writes:

> Catholics are now asking themselves, in the words of the Council, how other mystical traditions strive to penetrate "that ultimate mystery which engulfs our being, and whence we take our rise, and whither our journey leads us" (Declaration on Non-Christian Religions, n. 1). In doing so, they are guided by the Council's reminder that "the Catholic Church rejects nothing which is true and holy in these religions. She looks with sincere respect upon those ways of conduct and of life, those rules and teachings which, though differing in many particulars from what she holds and sets forth, nevertheless often reflect a ray of that Truth which enlightens all men" (id. 2). Not only must the Catholic scholar respect these other traditions and honestly evaluate the good contained in them, but the Council adds that he must "acknowledge, preserve and promote the spiritual and moral goods found among these men as well as the values in their society and culture."[47]

Thus, this active exploration of other faiths was a newly encouraged aspect of his Catholicism. This desire to learn more about other religions was not a sign that he was moving away from his Catholic faith, but rather he was adhering to the latest church teaching.

In addition, remarks Merton made at an interfaith conference in Calcutta approximately a month before he died clearly show his rootedness in the Christian faith, as well as a desire to be enriched by other traditions:

> I speak as a Western monk who is pre-eminently concerned with his own monastic calling and dedication . . . I need not add that I think we have now reached a stage (long overdue) of religious maturity at which it may be possible for someone to remain perfectly faithful to a Christian and Western monastic commitment, and yet to learn in depth from, say, a Buddhist discipline and experience.[48]

Merton was also an early pioneer of ecumenical work, organizing a retreat at Gethsemani to learn from non-Catholics who were committed to peace. While this sort of gathering is taken for granted in the twenty-first century, in 1964, bringing together Catholics, Quakers, Mennonites, Unitarians, Presbyterians, and Methodists was new. Over the course of three days, they discussed conscientious objection to war, the challenge of

---

47. Merton, *Mystics and Zen Masters*, viii–ix.
48. Merton, *Asian Journal*, xxiii.

technology, and a provocative question Merton raised: "By what right do we protest?"[49]

Merton and Zen

When it comes to exploring other faiths, Merton is best known for his exploration of Buddhism, and Zen in particular. He was one of the earliest prominent Catholic figures to begin the work of earnest dialogue between the two traditions. His interest was sparked by reading the works of D. T. Suzuki. While Merton read other Zen authors Suzuki was his main source for understanding it. Merton held him in such high esteem that he equated him with Einstein and Gandhi in terms of important figures of that time.[50] In addition, Merton writes that it was after reading Suzuki that he finally understood Buddhism and Zen, "whereas before it had been a very mysterious and confusing jumble of words, images, doctrines, legends, rituals, buildings, and so forth."[51] In fact, he states that Suzuki's works in English are "without question the most complete and most authentic presentation of an Asian tradition and experience by any one man in terms accessible to the West."[52]

It is important to point out that Merton did not view Zen as another religious system competing with his own Christianity. Instead, he states that it

> can shine through this or that system, religious or irreligious, just as light can shine through glass that is blue, or green, or red, or yellow. If Zen has any preference it is for glass that is plain, has no color, and is "just glass." In other words, to regard Zen merely and exclusively as Zen Buddhism is to falsify it and, no doubt, to betray the fact that one has no understanding of it whatever.[53]

Merton wrote two books during this period that are some of the best sources to examine his understanding of Zen. In *Mystics and Zen Masters*, published in 1967, and *Zen and the Birds of Appetite*, published in 1968, Merton lays out his understanding of Zen and why he finds it to be so

---

49. Oyer, *Pursuing the Spiritual Roots of Protest*, xii.
50. Merton, *Zen and the Birds of Appetite*, 59.
51. Merton, *Zen and the Birds of Appetite*, 60.
52. Merton, *Zen and the Birds of Appetite*, 62.
53. Merton, *Zen and the Birds of Appetite*, 4.

appealing. In Zen Merton was attracted to what he believed was a way to directly experience reality—"pure experience on a metaphysical level"[54]—without any need of external mediation, intellectualization, logical formulations, or even any kind of verbalization.[55] He describes it as a concrete and "lived ontology which explains itself not as theoretical propositions but in acts that come out of a certain quality of consciousness and awareness."[56] Zen does not lend itself to logical analysis. It is not a method of meditation or kind of spirituality. As Merton describes, it is "a 'way' and an 'experience,' a 'life,' but the way is paradoxically 'not a way.'"[57] Zen is not by any means a simple withdrawal from the material world to some kind of interior world of spirit. For Merton, Zen is in some sense entirely beyond the scope of psychological observation and metaphysical reflection, and, as he puts it, "for want of a better term, we may call it 'purely spiritual.'"[58] Here Merton is affirming that in Zen one can gain insights into the true nature of our being through living, and not by adhering to the strictures of a dogmatic religious belief.

Merton believed that Zen is an awareness potentially already present in every person, but the individual is not conscious of it. In addition, this direct or pure experience attained through Zen is not some kind of transcendent experience, where one is imbued with a feeling or realization of some awareness that comes from outside the individual. As Merton writes, "Zen is then not Kerygma but realization, not revelation but consciousness, not news from the Father who sends His Son into this world, but awareness of the ontological ground of our own being here and now, right in the midst of the world."[59] In this way, Merton believed that Zen does not teach anything; rather it points to a direct or pure awareness of living.[60] In Zen Merton sought to reach outside the boundaries of his own faith tradition while still standing squarely in it.

---

54. Merton, *Zen and the Birds of Appetite*, 43.
55. Merton, *Zen and the Birds of Appetite*, 37.
56. Merton, *Mystics and Zen Masters*, ix–x.
57. Merton, *Mystics and Zen Masters*, 12.
58. Merton, *Mystics and Zen Masters*, 14.
59. Merton, *Zen and the Birds of Appetite*, 47.
60. Merton, *Zen and the Birds of Appetite*, 48.

Cargo Cults

Merton also explored other faiths, including Hinduism, Islam, as well as the beliefs of indigenous peoples. I want to highlight one belief system that on its face may seem to have nothing in common with Merton's Catholicism—Cargo Cults. Merton didn't just engage with other religions that were congruent with his own. His study of Cargo Cults exemplifies his ability to search for the truth everywhere and find common ground with those who were seemingly dissimilar.

Cargo Cults refer to religious movements found primarily in native populations of colonized parts of the South Sea Islands, Africa, and Southeast Asia.[61] These indigenous peoples watched as their colonial rulers had mass-produced food and assorted luxury goods delivered as part of cargo shipments. Most of these items were meant to be consumed by the colonizers and not the colonized. Thus, the idea of cargo took on greater symbolic significance for some of the native population. It became, "the coming of a good time, when one would be like the whites and enjoy what the whites enjoyed—the coming of the millennium."[62] For a native, obtaining one's own cargo "would mean readmission to the human race. It would show him worthy of recognition as an equal to the white man. The problem was, therefore, one of identity, the native's place in the scheme of things, his human reality."[63]

These natives actively sought cargo of their own, and in order to learn how to acquire these goods

> observed the white man busying himself with great fuss over the papers in his office. He saw the white man sitting on his porch and never, at least not in the native's terms, doing very much work. In fact, the white man did not seem to do anything except strut around giving orders and signing papers, and then pretty soon a boat appeared, from across the sea, full of cargo.[64]

Since the logistical details of how these items were ordered and delivered was never explained to the native people some created their own mythical explanation for how the cargo came into being. As Merton writes, some believed these cargo shipments "had been magically fashioned by the white

---

61. I will use Merton's understanding of these groups when describing them.
62. Merton, *Love and Living*, 81.
63. Merton, *Love and Living*, 81.
64. Merton, *Love and Living*, 81.

man's dead ancestors from across the sea, with whom the white man had the secret of keeping in touch."[65] Based on their observations and limited understanding, natives developed a number of rituals in the hopes of securing cargo for themselves. For example, a group in New Guinea noticed that many colonial families kept fresh flowers in their homes. Believing that these flowers were some kind of prerequisite for receiving cargo they began to decorate their houses and whole villages with enormous amounts of them, hoping cargo would then come to them as well.

Merton points to an iconoclastic impulse that is found in many of these groups. There was a belief that the past must be repudiated as an act of faith in order to receive the cargo which would then usher in a new way of living. Merton describes how one group in Melanesia destroyed their property, crops, and even livestock in the belief that their sacrifice, and breaking ties with their old way of life, would be rewarded with cargo.

Merton understood that many in the West viewed these kinds of practices as "a curious aberration, an irrational and crazed manifestation of a purely primitive mentality, the sort of ignorance we have long since left behind us."[66] However, he dug deeper to find a shared perspective and common ground, writing that "a true understanding of Cargo mentality can tell us much about ourselves."[67]

Merton chronicles how each individual group eventually collapses when the faithful realize that, despite their best efforts, the cargo isn't coming. However, this process often starts up again in a slightly new form and the cycle repeats itself. Merton points to research that argues that this process: conversion, belief, commitment, sacrifice, breaking with the past, and ritual preparation for a new and better future, meets a deep human need. He believes this process occurs everywhere, "it is a basic myth-dream pattern common to everyone, including those who imagine themselves civilized."[68]

Merton states that because of their "exotic, often bizarre systems of ritualistic behavior"[69] it would be easy to assume members of these belief systems have nothing in common with Western Christians. However, he contends "we ought to ask ourselves if some of our own Western social and political movements are not, in fact, very similar to Cargo Cults, though

65. Merton, *Love and Living*, 82.
66. Merton, *Love and Living*, 83.
67. Merton, *Love and Living*, 83.
68. Merton, *Love and Living*, 86.
69. Merton, *Love and Living*, 80.

perhaps less naive."[70] Merton points out that Americans have created the elaborate myth of consumerism that promises a better life if we just keep buying the right products. As he writes "if you do not consume the new products fast, you are going to be left behind."[71] If that happens, all that our materialist culture promises to deliver, e.g., happiness, belonging, sex appeal—the "cargo" of modern America—will not be delivered. Merton was able to learn from those with which, on the surface, he did not share much in common. In so doing, he was able to gain better perspective on his own faith.

Merton and Camus

Merton did not just try to learn from those who had some kind of religious inclination. His interest in writer Albert Camus, a prominent critic of Christianity, shows that Merton could also find common ground with people who espoused no religious faith.

Camus's writings had a tremendous impact on Merton, with one biographer declaring "it would be hard to imagine the mature Thomas Merton without considering the full extent of Camus' influence."[72] Merton describes Camus as "perhaps one of the most serious and articulate ethical thinkers of the mid 20th century."[73] Merton was so taken with Camus that he wrote seven essays about him between 1966 and 1968.

Merton does not consider Camus to be an atheist, but instead describes him as being agnostic. He notes that Camus was no stranger to Christianity. In fact, Merton points out that while at the University of Algiers Camus wrote a thesis on early Christianity, Neoplatonism, Gnosticism, and St. Augustine.[74]

For Camus, the kind of Christianity he had encountered "was entirely foreign to his life . . . he therefore could not really identify himself with Christians."[75] Merton points out that Camus thought that belief in God was an intellectual copout based on his contention that life was absurd. That is, humanity has always searched for the meaning of existence and Camus

70. Merton, *Love and Living*, 80.
71. Merton, *Love and Living*, 84.
72. Cooper, *Thomas Merton's Art of Denial*, 209.
73. Merton, *Literary Essays of Thomas Merton*, 232.
74. Merton, *Literary Essays of Thomas Merton*, 184.
75. Merton, *Literary Essays of Thomas Merton*, 182.

posited that no reliable answers can ever be obtained. This absurdity arises from the perpetual search for answers that can never be found. Camus believed that many turned to God in an effort to resolve this absurdity.[76] Merton writes that for Camus, belief in God was "to choose an *explanation* and hence to evade the bitter honesty of a full confrontation with the absurd without hope and 'without appeal' to any force other than that of human honesty and courage within the confines of human limitation."[77]

Camus was critical of Christianity. For example, in his book, *The Plague*, he takes to task those members of the Catholic clergy who stress dogma over compassion. However, Merton writes that "if Camus is severe with Christians, it is because he thinks they have abdicated their mission of opposing the Plague and have instead devoted their talents to excusing and justifying it in terms of an ambiguous theology or . . . by compromise with political absolutism."[78] Later, Merton comments that Camus is reacting to a degraded and hollowed out form of "Christian morality" that had developed in Western societies and which tended to preserve so-called Christian values "by embalming them instead of allowing them to renew their own intrinsic life."[79]

Despite Camus's criticism of Christianity, Merton finds areas of agreement between Camus's writings and his own Christian faith. He notes that Camus's thought was rooted in a kind of humanism that affirmed the value and dignity of the individual, which is also a hallmark of Christianity. However, for Camus this was "in defiance of suffering and death . . . and the solidarity of men in revolt against the absurd, men whose comradeship has a certain purity because it is based on the renunciation of all illusions, all misleading ideals, all deceptive and hypocritical social forms."[80]

In commenting on Camus's famous work, *The Myth of Sisyphus*, Merton argues that the recognition of the absurd should not lead to nihilism. Instead, life should be "a revolt against negation, unhappiness and inevitable death."[81] Building on this, Merton goes on to say that after affirming the value of one's own life it is then possible to heed Christ's call to love others as you would yourself. In this way humanity can stand "in defiance of

---

76. Merton, *Literary Essays of Thomas Merton*, 236.
77. Merton, *Literary Essays of Thomas Merton*, 248.
78. Merton, *Literary Essays of Thomas Merton*, 183.
79. Merton, *Literary Essays of Thomas Merton*, 202.
80. Merton, *Literary Essays of Thomas Merton*, 186.
81. Merton, *Literary Essays of Thomas Merton*, 197.

an absurd philosophy or social system which, at any moment, may decree that they are to be killed in war, executed, exiled, or in some way ostracized, disgraced, and repudiated for defying the generally accepted myths."[82]

Merton concludes that Camus can be called a "'religious' thinker in so far as he affirms an ultimate faith. It is not a religious one but instead is a faith in man, a faith in revolt itself, a faith in the value of an existential witness which says 'no' to the absurd."[83] While seeking areas of agreement, Merton did not go so far as to say that Camus was a secret Christian. However, he did write that "a Christian is free, if he likes, to understand Camus in a Christian sense which Camus himself did not realize."[84] Even though Camus was a staunch critic of Christianity, Merton was able to move past the areas of disagreement to find common ground.

Breaking Down Silos

Merton was intellectually curious his entire life. He read voraciously on a number of subjects, including world literature, Western and Eastern theology, psychology, and anthropology. While committed to his life as a Catholic priest, monk, and writer, he made efforts to seek out other points of view. He was a prolific letter writer, corresponding with thousands of people about a wide variety of topics. He recognized the need to reach beyond our own experience and assumed worldview. As he writes:

> We hopefully look forward not to an age of eclecticism and syncretism, certainly, but to an age of understanding and adaptation that will be able to synthesize and make use of all that is good and noble in all the traditions of the past. If the world is to survive and if civilization is to endure or rather perhaps weather its present crisis and recover its dimension of "wisdom," we must hope for a new world culture that takes account of all civilized philosophies. The Christian scholar is obligated by his sacred vocation to understand and even preserve the heritage of all the great traditions insofar as they contain truths that cannot be neglected and that offer precious insights into Christianity itself. As the monks of the Middle Ages and the scholastics of the thirteenth century preserved the cultural traditions of Greece and Rome and adapted what they found in Arabic philosophy and science, so we too have

---

82. Merton, *Literary Essays of Thomas Merton*, 198.
83. Merton, *Literary Essays of Thomas Merton*, 221.
84. Merton, *Literary Essays of Thomas Merton*, 202.

a far greater task before us. It is time that we begin to consider something of our responsibility.[85]

Merton recognized that engaging with people who hold differing views can be difficult. He warns that Christians should avoid "othering" those that hold contrary positions. Merton cautions that Christians should not make generalizations about those on the other side of an issue, and should not assume they are wicked, ignorant, or can "never be reasonable or well-intentioned, and hence need never be listened to."[86] He suggests that Christians can test the sincerity of their own position by asking if they're willing to learn something from their adversary. Merton describes that the resistance to others' ideas often comes from an insecurity in our own convictions, because "we fear that we may be 'converted'—or perverted—by a pernicious doctrine."[87] He goes on to write that by maintaining a mature open-mindedness, viewing things from a different perspective, including from those we ideologically oppose, "we discover our own truth in a new light and are able to understand our own ideal more realistically."[88]

Finally, it is also important to point out that while he was widely read and had a brilliant mind, Merton also had a real respect for experts and he sought them out whenever possible. His exploration of Zen and Buddhism serves as a perfect example. In the 1950s, after reading some recommended Buddhist texts, he contacted D. T. Suzuki and began a long relationship of correspondence that culminated in an in-person meeting in New York City. He also corresponded with and was visited by Vietnamese Buddhist Thich Nhat Hanh. Finally, at the end of his life, he traveled to Asia in part to meet with prominent Buddhist figures, including the Dalai Lama, who could explain their traditions to him.

The Individual Witness and Affirming the Truth Wherever It Is Found

All of Merton's efforts to break down silos, seek the truth, and work with those who are different from us to identify common ground can be instructive for Christians today. He remained faithful to his own Christian faith

---

85. Merton, *Mystics and Zen Masters*, 65.
86. Merton, *Nonviolent Alternative*, 211.
87. Merton, *Nonviolent Alternative*, 214.
88. Merton, *Nonviolent Alternative*, 214.

while exploring different ones, showing that openness to the ideas of others does not lead to abandoning one's own beliefs. For example, as I briefly discussed in chapter 3, Merton engaged with theological trends of his time, including the Death of God movement. While he was able to find common ground in some of its critiques of Christianity at that time, Merton ultimately rejected its main thesis.

Thomas Merton demonstrates that it is possible to actively seek out different points of view, motivated by a sincere desire to learn something. He was not engaging with others for the thrill of debate, nor was he seeking out new beliefs so he could jettison his old ones. Merton remained curious, humble, and open to learn from everyone, showing us how we can reach out beyond the confines of our own silo or tradition.

Conclusion

IN CONCLUDING THIS BOOK about how Thomas Merton can help us better engage with the world, it is important to note two issues that I chose not to address: the Coronavirus and war in the Ukraine. As I write, the pandemic continues, with variants emerging and producing new surges in cases. Reactions to COVID-19 have exposed the fissures of our fractured post-truth culture, with public health issues becoming politicized. Both sides of the political spectrum have dug in, with competing versions of the truth dictating positions on vaccines, mask usage, etc. Our society is returning to normal due to growing vaccination rates and restriction fatigue. However, I suspect that many of the attitudes and habits forged during the first two years of the pandemic will have a significant impact on some of the issues raised in this book. For example, how many members of religious denominations who regularly attended worship services prior to the pandemic will stick with their new routine of online worship? A January 2022 poll found that almost one-third of Catholics ages 18 to 35 expect to attend Mass less often than they did before the pandemic. In addition, 73 percent of them said that one can be a "good Catholic" without going to Mass regularly.[1] Because the pandemic is not over it's not possible to appreciate the full, long-term impact it is likely to have. Thus, I have resisted making many statements about it.

Second, Merton's peace writings took on renewed relevance and urgency when Russia invaded Ukraine. Both conservative and liberal media outlets regularly explore various "escalation scenarios," describing a series of events that could result in the use of nuclear weapons. Now the Millennial and iGen generations, who previously did not have to worry about the possibility of a nuclear war, sadly can now commiserate with older Americans

---

1. Sullivan, "Survey," para. 1.

who lived through the Cold War. This conflict serves as another example of how Merton's writings from a half century ago are still vitally important and relevant today. However, because this war is still being waged at the time of this writing, it is not possible to adequately address it.

In surveying Merton's work, I tried to focus on issues that are still relevant today and can help Christians better engage with our current post-Christian and post-truth world. This book is not meant to be the final word on any of these subjects, but instead it continues an ongoing conversation. Many fine books and articles have been written in the last few decades about various aspects of Merton's work and how they relate to the world today. Hopefully this small book furthers that dialogue in some way.

In exploring his writings, I looked at the larger arc of Merton's work over the last fifteen years of his life. This is important because his ideas and positions often changed. Merton recognized this trait in himself, writing "my ideas are always changing, always moving from one center, always seeing the center from somewhere else. I will always be accused of inconsistencies—and will no longer be there to hear the accusation."[2]

There are a number of different ways one may use Merton as a model for action, and I have only offered the broadest suggestions, knowing each individual can find specific opportunities to implement them. Merton is clear that we should not retreat from the broader secular world, and instead should fully engage with it and affirm all that is good. In addition, despite the growing trend to create one's own spirituality, using Merton as a guide means finding a faith community that both supports and challenges us. Merton also reminds us that it is normal to occasionally feel restless and that change does not necessarily cure that. Unfortunately, there is no shortage of suffering in the world. As such, there are many opportunities to join with those in our local communities who are in distress, and work with them to eliminate the root causes of that suffering. We can also join with our neighbors, physical or virtual, to give of our time and resources to work for peace and help those affected by war. Finally, each of us can assess the ways that our thinking is siloed and strive to openly engage with others, especially those that have different points of view, to find areas of agreement and the truth.

Merton recognized that the individual Christian witness would become even more important in a world in which the institutional church has less and less influence. The church will continue to offer guidance and

---

2. Merton, *Dancing in the Water of Life*, 5:67.

serve as an alternative to the vacuous elements of secular society. However, it can no longer affect change simply through fiat. Individual Christians, now more than ever, must put their faith into action.

Merton is clear that making real changes in the world will require us to disrupt the status quo. Change will be uncomfortably slow, and require us to confront ugly truths about our social and economic systems. Merton repeatedly warned against making token gestures that make us feel good but do nothing to address the root causes of our social ills. Using Merton as a guide is not a series of tasks to perform, it is an orientation. It is an attitude and orientation towards the world. It is a genuine attempt to see Christ in every other member of the human race. When we are able to do this, our differences fall away. Others' problems become our own, and our life is oriented to serve and learn from them.

A reader could rightly conclude that this is simply a call to "be a Christian." That is absolutely true! However, there is hardly one normative Christian experience. It is readily apparent today, in our post-truth world, that all Christians do not agree if they should, or how to, engage with the world. Increasingly, those from both ends of the political and ideological spectrum co-opt parts of Christianity to justify their own positions. Merton's life and writings can help reorient us.

It is easy to focus on all that is wrong in the world today, to lose hope, or to be pressed into inaction under the weight of its problems. That was certainly the case during Merton's lifetime. However, no matter how dire things looked, he remained hopeful. Merton reminds us that Christ found good in the world and redeemed it. Each generation of Christians is called to continue that task. Thomas Merton can inspire and guide us, doing the hard work of building God's kingdom on earth.

Bibliography

"America's Changing Religious Landscape." *Pew Research Center*, May 30, 2020. https://www.pewforum.org/2015/05/12/americas-changing-religious-landscape/.

Andersen, Kurt. *Fantasyland: How America Went Haywire: A 500-Year History*. New York: Random House, 2018.

Arnold, John H. *Belief and Unbelief in Medieval Europe*. London: Bloomsbury Academic, 2011.

Barber, Malcolm. *The Cathars in Languedoc: Dualist Heretics in Languedoc in the High Middle Ages*. London: Routledge, 2013.

Brooks, David. "The Benedict Option." *New York Times*, March 14, 2017. https://www.nytimes.com/2017/03/14/opinion/the-benedict-option.html.

Cadwalladr, Carole. "Daniel Dennett: 'I Begrudge Every Hour I Have to Spend Worrying about Politics.'" *The Guardian*, February 12, 2017. https://www.theguardian.com/science/2017/feb/12/daniel-dennett-politics-bacteria-bach-back-dawkins-trump-interview.

Carrón, Julián. *Disarming Beauty: Essays on Faith, Truth, and Freedom*. Notre Dame: University of Notre Dame Press, 2017.

Chaput, Charles J. *Strangers in a Strange Land: Living the Catholic Faith in a Post-Christian World*. New York: St. Martin's Griffin, 2017.

Cooper, David D. *Thomas Merton's Art of Denial: The Evolution of a Radical Humanist*. Athens: University of Georgia Press, 1989.

Dawkins, Richard. *The God Delusion*. New York: Houghton Mifflin Harcourt, 2008.

Dennett, Daniel C. *Breaking the Spell*. New York: Penguin, 2007.

Dreher, Rod. *The Benedict Option: A Strategy for Christians in a Post-Christian Nation*. New York: Sentinel, 2017.

Drescher, Elizabeth. *Choosing Our Religion: The Spiritual Lives of America's Nones*. New York: Oxford University Press, 2016.

Ellingson, Stephen. *The Megachurch and the Mainline: Remaking Religious Tradition in the Twenty-First Century*. Chicago: University of Chicago Press, 2007.

Festival of Faiths. "Thomas Merton and Race—Dr. Christopher Pramuk." *YouTube*, June 25, 2015. 20:05. https://www.youtube.com/watch?v=GHOd5bke3U4.

Forest, Jim. *The Root of War Is Fear: Thomas Merton's Advice to Peacemakers*. Maryknoll, NY: Orbis, 2016.

Frankfurt, Harry G. *On Bullshit*. Princeton: Princeton University Press, 2005.

———. *On Truth*. New York: Knopf, 2006.

Bibliography

Gardner, Fiona. *The Only Mind Worth Having: Thomas Merton and the Child Mind.* Eugene, OR: Cascade Books, 2015.

Giroux, Robert, and Thomas Merton. *The Letters of Robert Giroux and Thomas Merton.* Edited by Patrick H. Samway and Jonathan Montaldo. Notre Dame: University of Notre Dame Press, 2015.

Grayston, Donald. *Thomas Merton and the Noonday Demon: The Camaldoli Correspondence.* Eugene, OR: Cascade Books, 2015.

Gregory, Brad S. *The Unintended Reformation: How a Religious Revolution Secularized Society.* Cambridge: Belknap, 2015.

Harris, Sam. *The End of Faith: Religion, Terror and the Future of Reason.* London: Norton, 2005.

Higgins, Michael W. *Thomas Merton: Faithful Visionary.* Collegeville, MN: Liturgical, 2014.

Hitchens, Christopher. *God Is Not Great: How Religion Poisons Everything.* New York: Twelve, 2007.

Hitchens, Christopher, et al. *The Four Horsemen: The Conversation that Sparked an Atheist Revolution.* New York: Random House, 2019.

Hoffman, Jan. "How Anti-Vaccine Sentiment Took Hold in the United States." *New York Times,* September 23, 2019. https://www.nytimes.com/2019/09/23/health/anti-vaccination-movement-us.html.

Horan, Daniel P. *The Franciscan Heart of Thomas Merton: A New Look at the Spiritual Inspiration of His Life, Thought, and Writing.* Notre Dame: Ave Maria, 2014.

———. "Thomas Merton & Black Lives Matter: Spirituality and Racial Justice for Our Time." *YouTube,* September 9, 2020. 1:18:36. https://youtu.be/YhoCci2h-EQ.

"In U.S., Decline of Christianity Continues at Rapid Pace." *Pew Research Center,* October 17, 2019. https://www.pewforum.org/2019/10/17/in-u-s-decline-of-christianity-continues-at-rapid-pace/.

Kavanagh, Jennifer, and Michael D. Rich. *Truth Decay: An Initial Exploration of the Diminishing Role of Facts and Analysis in American Public Life.* Santa Monica, CA: Rand, 2018.

Kilde, Jeanne Halgren. *When Church Became Theater: The Transformation of Evangelical Architecture and Worship in Nineteenth-Century America.* New York: Oxford University Press, 2005.

Lipsey, Roger. *Make Peace before the Sun Goes Down: The Long Encounter of Thomas Merton and His Abbot, James Fox.* Boston: Shambhala, 2015.

McIntyre, Lee C. *Post-Truth.* Cambridge, MA: MIT Press, 2018.

McPhate, Mike, and Ben Sisario. "4 More Years: Rush Limbaugh Signs a New Radio Contract." *New York Times,* August 2, 2016. https://www.nytimes.com/2016/08/03/business/media/rush-limbaugh-renews-radio-contract.html.

"Megachurch Definition." *Hartford Institute for Religion Research.* http://hirr.hartsem.edu/megachurch/definition.html.

"Megachurches." *Christianity Today.* https://www.christianitytoday.com/ct/topics/m/megachurches/.

Mercadante, Linda A. *Belief without Borders: Inside the Minds of the Spiritual but Not Religious.* New York: Oxford University Press, 2014.

Merton, Thomas. *The Asian Journal of Thomas Merton.* Edited by Naomi Burton et al. New York: New Directions, 1975.

Bibliography

———. "The Christian in the World." *Learn25*, n.d. Merton Talks #4, 35:19. https://s3.amazonaws.com/NowYouKnowMedia/downloads/MertonTalks/04_MertonTalks_TheChristianInTheWorl.mp3.

———. *Cold War Letters*. Edited by Christine M. Bochen and William H. Shannon. Maryknoll, NY: Orbis, 2006.

———. *Conjectures of a Guilty Bystander*. Garden City, NY: Doubleday, 1966.

———. *Contemplation in a World of Action*. Notre Dame: University of Notre Dame Press, 2003.

———. *Dancing in the Water of Life: Seeking Peace in the Hermitage, 1963–1965*. Edited by Robert E. Daggy. Vol. 5. *Journals of Thomas Merton*. 7 vols. San Francisco: HarperSanFrancisco, 1997.

———. *Faith and Violence: Christian Teaching and Christian Practice*. Notre Dame: University of Notre Dame Press, 1968.

———. *The Hidden Ground of Love: The Letters of Thomas Merton on Religious Experience and Social Concerns*. Edited by William H. Shannon. San Diego: Harcourt Brace Jovanovich, 1985.

———. *Learning to Love: Exploring Solitude and Freedom*. Edited by Christine M. Bochen. Vol. 6. *Journals of Thomas Merton*. 7 vols. San Francisco: HarperSanFrancisco, 1997.

———. *Life and Holiness*. New York: Image, 2014.

———. *The Literary Essays of Thomas Merton*. Edited by Patrick Hart. New York: New Directions, 1985.

———. *Love and Living*. Edited by Patrick Hart and Naomi Burton Stone. New York: Farrar, Straus & Giroux, 1979.

———. "Merton Leaves for Asia: Bidding Farewell to Gethsemani." *Learn25*, n.d. Merton Talks #37, 42:18. https://s3.amazonaws.com/NowYouKnowMedia/downloads/MertonTalks/37_MertonTalks_Mastered.mp3.

———. "The Monk in the Diaspora." *New Blackfriars* 45.529–30 (1964) 290–302.

———. *Mystics and Zen Masters*. New York: Farrar, Strauss & Giroux, 1967.

———. *No Man Is an Island*. New York: Harcourt Brace, 1955.

———. *The Nonviolent Alternative*. Edited by Gordon C. Zahn. New York: Farrar, Straus & Giroux, 1987.

———. *The Other Side of the Mountain: The End of the Journey*. Edited by Patrick Hart. Vol. 7. *The Journals of Thomas Merton*. 7 vols. San Francisco: HarperSanFrancisco, 1998.

———. *Peace in the Post-Christian Era*. Maryknoll, NY: Orbis, 2006.

———. *Run to the Mountain: The Story of a Vocation*. Edited by Patrick Hart. Vol. 1. *Journals of Thomas Merton*. 7 vols. San Francisco: HarperSanFrancisco, 1995.

———. *A Search for Solitude: Pursuing the Monk's True Life*. Edited by Lawrence S. Cunningham. New York: HarperOne, 2009.

———. *The Secular Journal of Thomas Merton*. New York: Farrar, Straus & Giroux, 1959.

———. *Seeds of Destruction*. New York: Farrar, Straus & Giroux, 1987.

———. *The Seven Storey Mountain*. San Diego: Harcourt Brace Jovanovich, 1976.

———. *Sign of Jonas*. New York: Harcourt, Brace, 1953.

———. "Thich Nhat Hanh and the Spiritual Crisis of the Vietnam War." *Learn25*, n.d. Merton Talks #25, 37:47. https://s3.amazonaws.com/NowYouKnowMedia/downloads/MertonTalks/25_MertonTalks_ThichNhatHanh.mp3.

Bibliography

———. *Turning Towards the World (1960–1963): The Pivotal Years*. Edited by Victor A. Kramer. Vol. 4. *Journals of Thomas Merton*. 7 vols. San Francisco: HarperSanFrancisco, 1997.

———. "Two Conferences on Prayer: India 1968." In *Merton Annual: Studies in Culture, Spirituality and Social Concerns*, edited by Deborah Pope Kehoe and Joseph Quinn Raab, 31:17–40. 31 vols. Louisville: Fons Vitae, 2018.

———. *Witness to Freedom: The Letters of Thomas Merton in Times of Crisis*. Edited by William H. Shannon. New York: Farrar, Straus & Giroux, 1985.

———. *Zen and the Birds of Appetite*. New York: New Directions, 1968.

Merton, Thomas, and Ernesto Cardenal. *From the Monastery to the World: The Letters of Thomas Merton and Ernesto Cardenal*. Edited by Jessie Sandoval. Translated by Jeffrey Neilson. Berkeley: Counterpoint, 2018.

Miller, Donald Earl. *Reinventing American Protestantism: Christianity in the New Millennium*. Berkeley: University of California Press, 1999.

Moore, Robert Laurence. *Selling God American Religion in the Marketplace of Culture*. New York: Oxford University Press, 1994.

Moses, John. *Divine Discontent: The Prophetic Voice of Thomas Merton*. London: Bloomsbury, 2014.

Mott, Michael. *The Seven Mountains of Thomas Merton*. Boston: Houghton Mifflin, 1984.

Nichols, Tom. *The Death of Expertise: The Campaign against Established Knowledge and Why It Matters*. New York: Oxford University Press, 2017.

"'Nones' On the Rise." *Pew Research Center*, October 9, 2012. https://www.pewresearch.org/religion/2012/10/09/nones-on-the-rise/.

Orberson, David. *Thomas Merton—Evil and Why We Suffer: From Purified Soul Theodicy to Zen*. Eugene, OR: Cascade, 2018.

"Outreach 100 List." *Outreach Magazine*, January 10, 2019. https://outreachmagazine.com/outreach-100-list.html#/list/2018/all.

Oyer, Gordon. *Pursuing the Spiritual Roots of Protest*. Eugene, OR: Cascade, 2014.

Park, Jaechan Anselmo. *Thomas Merton's Encounter with Buddhism and Beyond: His Interreligious Dialogue, Inter-Monastic Exchanges, and Their Legacy*. Collegeville, MN: Liturgical, 2019.

Pollan, Michael. *How to Change Your Mind: What the New Science of Psychedelics Teaches Us about Consciousness, Dying, Addiction, Depression, and Transcendence*. New York: Penguin, 2019.

"Religious Congregations in 21st Century America." National Congregations Study, December 2015. https://sites.duke.edu/ncsweb/files/2019/02/NCSIII_report_final.pdf.

Rice, Edward. *The Man in the Sycamore Tree: The Good Times and Hard Life of Thomas Merton*. San Diego: Harcourt Brace Jovanovich, 1985.

Rider, Catherine. *Magic and Religion in Medieval England*. London: Reaktion, 2012.

Roper, Lyndal. *Martin Luther: Renegade and Prophet*. New York: Random House, 2017.

Russell, Bob, with Rusty Russell. *When God Builds a Church: 10 Principles for Growing a Dynamic Church, the Remarkable Story of Southeast Christian Church*. New York: Howard, 2000.

Shannon, William H. *Silent Lamp: The Thomas Merton Story*. New York: Crossroad, 1996.

Smith, Christian, and Melinda Lundquist Denton. *Soul Searching: The Religious and Spiritual Lives of American Teenagers*. New York: Oxford University Press, 2011.

Bibliography

Southeast Christian Church. "Moving from Religion to Relationship | Dave Stone." *YouTube*, November 19, 2018. 33:34. https://youtu.be/F50GouskGhU.

Sullivan, Robert David. "Survey: A Third of Young Catholics Expect to Attend Mass Less Often after the Pandemic." *America*, November 10, 2021. https://www.americamagazine.org/faith/2021/11/10/cara-survey-young-american-catholics-241803.

Tavris, Carol, and Elliot Aronson. *Mistakes Were Made (but Not by Me): Why We Justify Foolish Beliefs, Bad Decisions and Hurtful Acts*. New York: Mariner, 2020.

Taylor, Mark C. *After God*. Chicago: University of Chicago Press, 2009.

Thumma, Scott, and Warren Bird. "Recent Shifts in America's Largest Protestant Churches: Megachurches 2015 Report." *Hartford Institute for Religion Research*, 2000. http://hirr.hartsem.edu/megachurch/2015_Megachurches_Report.pdf.

Thumma, Scott, and Dave Travis. *Beyond Megachurch Myths: What We Can Learn from America's Largest Churches*. San Francisco: Jossey-Bass, 2007.

Vahanian, Gabriel. *Wait Without Idols: Understanding the God that Kills Himself*. Eugene, OR: Wipf & Stock, 2010.

Veith, Gene Edward. *Post-Christian: A Guide to Contemporary Thought and Culture*. Wheaton, IL: Crossway, 2020.

Walters, Kerry S. *Revolutionary Deists: Early America's Rational Infidels*. Amherst, NY: Prometheus, 2011.

Weis, Rene. *The Yellow Cross: The Story of the Last Cathars' Rebellion against the Inquisition, 1290–1329*. New York: Vintage, 2002.

Wilber, Ken. *Trump and a Post-Truth World*. Boulder, CO: Shambhala, 2017.

Wilkes, Paul. *Merton: By Those Who Knew Him Best*. San Francisco: Harper & Row, 1987.

Zahn, Gordon C. "Original Child Monk: An Appreciation." In *The Nonviolent Alternative*, by Thomas Merton, edited by Gordon C. Zahn, iv–xli. New York: Farrar, Straus & Giroux, 1987.

Index

Andersen, Kurt, 38
atheism, 12, 15–18, 72, 77

Baez, Joan, 62
Bennett, Tom, 47–48
Berrigan, Daniel, 62, 72
Brahmachari, Mahanambrata, 50
Burns, Dom Flavian, 63
Burton, Naomi, 51
bullshit, 37–38

Camus, Albert, 113–15
Cardenal, Ernesto, 81–83
Carrón, Julian, 75–76
Cathars, 7–8
Colbert, Stephen, 30
Cold War Letters, 105

Daggy, Robert, 56
Dalai Lama, 64–65, 116
Dawkins, Richard, 15–17
Day, Dorothy, 62
death of expertise, 35–37
Deism, 10
Dennett, Daniel, 15–16, 40
Denton, Melinda Lundquist, 25, 27, 29
Dreher, Rod, 74–75
Dresher, Elizabeth, 12–13
Dunne, Dom Frederick, 54

Ellingson, Stephen, 25
Enlightenment, 5, 9–10, 18, 38

Forest, Jim, 104

Fox, Dom James, 57–59, 61–62, 81–83, 104
Frankfurt, Harry, 37

Giabani, Dom Aselmo, 80
Gregory, Brad S., 9
Griffin, John Howard, 62

Harris, Sam, 15–16
Hearst, William, 32
Hitchens, Christopher, 17–18

Jenkins, Martha "Bonnemaman," 44–46, 50
Jenkins, Samuel "Pop," 44–47, 50
just war theory, 97–98

Kavanagh, Jennifer, 32–33
Kearns, Joe Rex, 19

Luther, Martin, 8, 21
Lynch, Olivia, ix

McCarthy, Jenny, 36
McIntyre, Lee, 31, 39
magic, 6–7
Marty, Martin, 71–72
megachurches, 11, 18–22, 24–25, 29
Mercadante, Linda A., 13–14
Merton, John Paul, 44–47, 54
Merton, Owen, 44–47
Merton, Ruth, 44–46
Merton, Thomas
    affair with M, 61–62

Index

(Merton, Thomas continued)
   assessment of the secular world, 67–68
   assessment of the state of religion, 68, 70–71
      Death of God, 69–70, 117
   Asian trip, 63–66, 116
   Camaldoli order, 56, 80–81
   Cargo Cults, 111–13
   Carthusian order, 56, 79–80
   childhood, 44–47
   church in diaspora, 72–73
   college years, 47–50
   death, 66
   early monastic life, 53–55
   experience at Fourth and Walnut, 59–60, 65
   experience at Mass in Havana, Cuba, 51, 65
   experience at Polonnaruwa, 65–66
   Franciscan order, 51
   hermitage years, 61–63, 83–84
   mental health, 55–56, 60, 82
   nuclear war, 42, 71, 83, 96, 99–100, 102–4, 118
   pacifism, 96–98
   paternity issue, 48–49, 51
   physical health, 46–47, 53, 56, 61
   quest to find home, 79–84
   racism, 87–94
   Vietnam War, 62, 96–97, 100–101, 103
   writing about peace, 104–5
   Young Communist League, 49
Miller, Donald, 22
Moore, R. Laurence, 21
Moralistic Therapeutic Deism, 28–29, 72
Mott, Michael, 44, 55
Mystics and Zen Masters, 109

Nhat Hanh, Thich, 62, 97, 116
Nichols, Tom, 35–36
No Man Is an Island, 86
Nones, 1, 11–15, 22, 24–25, 29, 85

Offitt, Paul A., 36

Pasternak, Boris, 62
Peace in the Post-Christian Era, 104–5,
postmodernism, 39–40
post-Christian, 1–2, 5, 29–30, 40, 69–70, 74
post-truth, 1, 30–35, 38–40, 74, 119–20
Pramuk, Christopher, 107
Protestant Reformation, 5–6, 8–9
Pulitzer, Joseph, 32

Rahner, Karl, 62, 72
Rice, Ed, 48
Rich, Michael D., 32–33
Rider, Catherine, 6–7
Ruether, Rosemary Radford, 62
Russell, Bob, 19

Scott, Evelyn, 45–46
Sign of Jonas, 80
Smith, Christian, 25, 27, 29
Sortais, Dom Gabriel, 58
Southeast Christian Church, 19–20, 22–24
Stone, Dave, 22–24
Suzuki, D.T., 62, 109, 116

Taylor, Mark C., 8–9
The Seven Storey Mountain, 55, 79–80
Thirty Poems, 54
Thumma, Scott, 19
Travis, Dave, 19
Trump, Donald, 38

Vahanian, Gabriel, 69
Vatican II, 88, 108

Wakefield, Andrew, 36
Walsh, Dan, 51–52
Walters, Kerry S., 10
Wygal, Jim, 60

Zahn, Gordon, C., 95
Zen, 42, 60, 109–10, 116
Zen and the Birds of Appetite, 109

128